So Long for Now

So Long for Now

A World War II Memoir

William M. Dwyer

Edited by Marge Dwyer
Lawrenceville, New Jersey

Copyright © 2009 by William M. Dwyer.

ISBN: Hardcover   978-1-4415-4404-9
             Softcover   978-1-4415-4403-2

All rights reserved. No part of this book may be reproduced or transmitted in any form or by any means, electronic or mechanical, including photocopying, recording, or by any information storage and retrieval system, without permission in writing from the copyright owner.

This book was printed in the United States of America.

To order additional copies of this book, contact:
Xlibris Corporation
1-888-795-4274
www.Xlibris.com
Orders@Xlibris.com

For Hall and Charley
Ours was the past
Yours is the future

Acknowledgments

An immense thank you to John Timpane for editorial input; to readers Suzy Dwyer, Linda Levy, Mary Jane Aklonis, and Areta Parle for their ongoing help and encouragement; to Betsy Keuffel for hours and hours of technological support and editorial suggestions without which this book would never have been published; and finally and especially to Bill Dwyer who told it like it was.

CONTENTS

Foreword .... *xiii*

Prologue *1*

PART I

Growing up Irish Catholic 3
    The Early Years 4
    572 Bellevue 10
    The Altar Boy from Trenton, New Jersey 16
    The Crossing 29
    The Golden Age of Tennis 36
    College Days 42
    The Newspaper Business 45

PART II

The War 51
    Glamour Boy Aviator 52
    I Become a Spy 66
    Normandy 71
    Saint-Lo 81
    Paris 87
    Belgium 89
    Reporting the War Scene 107
    The Hemingways 110
    Rothenburg 118
    Dachau 133
    End of the War 138

PART III

Anthology of Selected Columns and Profiles 145
    Dorothy Commins, People You Meet Along the Way, ... 145
    Charles S. Gilpin, The Original 'Emperor Jones,' 148
    Breakfast at the White House, ... 151
    Writing at Home, ... 155
    Hugh Kahler, A Reformed Second-rater
    Finds Success as a Writer, ... 160
    Peter Benchley, 'Jaws' 164
    Dawes' Debut, 50 Years in the Making, ... 168
    John McPhee, 'Levels of the Game' 175
    Notes for a Future Historian, ... 178
    Ann Packard, Portrait of the Artist as Woman, ... 188
    The Minuet in G and Me, ... 195
    The Last Mile, Pray for Us, ... 198
    Albert Herpin, The Man who Never Slept, ... 201
    Leicester Hemingway, Memories of Les, ... 205
    Personal Notes: Clinical Depression Waylays
    Unsuspecting Stroke Victim 211
    JP Miller, Reviewing the Life of Writer—and Friend, ... 216
    Dwyer Addictions, ... 219
    Golfing with Dad, ... 222

PART IV

The Endgame 225

Foreword

If Ernest Hemingway were alive today, he could write this introduction because he spent some of his most interesting days with Bill Dwyer during WWII. But only a small part of *So Long For Now* concerns Hemingway; the rest of it is a series of vignettes from a charming and full life. Charming whether actually lived or made up—like the cherry pie incident—and well worth reading. Bill was a storyteller and told stories about sports, about politics, about neighborhoods, and about things which popped into his mind. Only way to share these precious experiences is to read this book.

Brendan T. Byrne
Former Governor of New Jersey
February 2009

Prologue

The genesis of this book goes back to the day in 1971 when my wife Marjorie gave birth to our one and only child, Suzanna. I was 53 years old at the time, and in the ensuing years I began to wonder about the gap that would exist between Suzy and me at age 15, when I would be 68. I felt it incumbent upon me to bridge the gap and one of the ways to do so would be to tell her something about the world I grew up in.

I am writing this knowing I'll be dead before I can tell Suzy some of the things she might like to know about the life and times of her father. One of the stories will be about my 2½ years in the Army. Another will be about my being more of an observer than a participant in the journey through life. Another will be the people I remember on the journey: Les Hemingway, Oliver Goldsmith, Ernest Hemingway, J. D. Salinger, and so many others.

My Dad never got over the wonder of television. I'll never get over the wonder of Suzy—Suzanna Duncan Dwyer. Just watched her ride off on her bike to Jimmy Kuser's down the street. "M'wah, Love ya," she said as usual, blowing a kiss to her mother as she hopped aboard the bike in shorts, T-shirt, and jogging sneakers. Her face tanned, blonder than ever before.

So, Suzy, here goes.

WMD 1982

PART I

Growing up Irish Catholic

To understand my war experience is first to know the Dwyers as a family. Growing up in Trenton, we were Irish Catholics first, Americans second.

A large part of our lives revolved around the church. My mother went to mass every day of her life until just before she died, when a stroke made it impossible. Throughout the many trials of her life, she never blamed God or questioned why. Her faith carried her through.

I started out that way, too.

The Early Years

*Paternal Grandparents with sons
James and Edward*

It is of record that on Thursday, October 10, 1889, in a small house on Jefferson Street in Trenton, New Jersey, a son, to be named Edward T. Dwyer, was born to William Dwyer, a potter, his wife, Catherine, nee Corcoran. By the early 1900s, Edward and his brother James were orphans. Very little is known about the death of their parents except that they are buried in St. John's Cemetery. Father William Henry Dwyer died in 1904; mother Catherine Corcoran, born in Kilkenny, Ireland, died in 1907. The boys were, for a while, wards of the Swetnam family—distant relatives—who owned Sanitary Earthenware, a company that would have bankrolled the boys' college education at Notre Dame, but the company went bankrupt and so went their dream.

One day early in the year 1914, Edward T. Dwyer visited the pastor of St. Mary's Cathedral in downtown Trenton, to arrange a date for his marriage to Anna Ellen Larkin, a parishioner of St. Joseph's Church, in the northern section of Trenton. The priest scheduled the wedding date, but only after posing this question: "Aren't the girls in your own parish good enough for you?"

My parents on their wedding day

Another bit of family history centered on Bridget Hanlon, an ancestor of ours, who ran an "actors' boarding house" on North Warren Street. Buster and the rest of the Keatons, who often performed at the Trent Theater down the street, were frequent guests. So were Eddie Cantor, George Jessel, and Al Jolson, then struggling performers.

Some of the "permanent" guests spent their final days at the boarding house, and Aunt Bridget sometimes had to make room for their burial in the plot that contained the remains of her husband. At one point it became necessary to dig up her husband's casket to make room for yet another boarder who had died broke.

This prompted a question to Bridget: When her husband's casket was taken up, had she looked inside?

Yes, Bridget confessed, she had.

And how did he look?

Her answer: "Just a little dusty."

My mother's family, the Larkins, was descended from Mary Kelly, who had come alone to America from Ireland at the age of 15, having secured the passage money by winning first prize at a lace exposition. As the story goes, she met her future husband, Michael Hart, while walking down a country road in Jobstown, New Jersey, where she was living. Earlier that year, Michael had escaped from a chain gang in Johnstown, Pennsylvania, to which he had been shanghaied right off the boat from Ireland.

They eventually married, raised a family, and remained in the area until their deaths. One of their children was Ellen Hart, my mother's mother. Michael was known for his playful sense of humor. Every morning while shaving, he reportedly called out, "Mary Kelly, you married yourself a handsome man."

On September 20, 1916, Edward and Anna (called Nan) had the first of their five children: me.

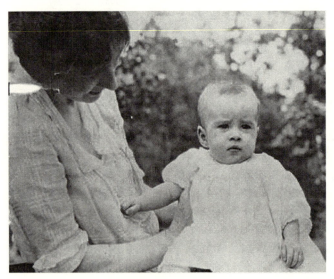

Mother and me

I was born not in a hospital, but at home on Evans Avenue in Trenton. This was five or six blocks north of the family business, the Dwyer Brothers stationery store, 127 North Broad Street.

A year or two later we moved to the 700 block of Stuyvesant Avenue, in the western section of the city, a short distance from Sprague's Hardware, and across the street from Gran'mom, Mrs. Ellen (Hart) Larkin, my mother's mother.

Gran'mom

Later I kidded her by calling her Ellie. She had the brightest smile. I will never forget the picture of her reading the *New Egypt Press* with two *Woolworth Five & Dime* specs perched on her nose and an enlarging glass. When I was older, I took her to Division Street in East Trenton to collect rents of $15 a month from each the five or six houses she owned.

I wrote a column about our family connection in Ireland.

Looking back to 1926
The Trenton Times, Early 1970s

One Sunday morning in the spring of 1920, my father, Edward T. Dwyer, and his brother, James W., took the train from Trenton to New York to meet their cousin, James Corcoran. Corcoran was due to arrive by ship from Ireland. Or so the brothers expected.

The Dwyers had opened their store on North Broad Street in downtown Trenton about a decade earlier, in March 1911.

Uncle Jim and Dad at their store

Before that, my father had worked, first as a delivery boy for Long's Drug Store at East State and Chambers Streets, and later as a clerk in Applegate's Sporting Goods at East State between Warren and Broad. His younger brother, Jim, had worked in several places, including Steve Haley's market.

The brothers, each in their early 20s, had taken a business course at Rider College and had borrowed about $500 from the Trenton Trust to establish Dwyer Brothers, stationers and office outfitters, at 127 North Broad Street. Through the years they had done well enough, making the rent on time and discounting their bills. As their train rattled on toward Manhattan, they wondered if their cousin would be settling in Trenton and perhaps working at the store. He was a nephew of their late mother, Catherine Corcoran Dwyer.

At this point the story of that Sunday in 1920 becomes a bit hazy. The one thing clear is that no ship arrived that day with their cousin aboard. There was apparently a misunderstanding about the date. Perhaps their cousin had already landed and, finding no one to greet him, had sought his fortune elsewhere.

Some months or perhaps years later, the Dwyer brothers learned that their cousin had gone west. They corresponded occasionally with the Corcoran family in Ireland, but none of the letters is to be found today, except one written by James Corcoran's sister on June 13, 1931:

> I am sure you will be surprised to receive a letter from me. We often spoke about you both and wondered do you ever think about the Corcoran family?
>
> I am sure you will be sorry to hear that poor Jim was shot in Chicago on the 25th November last. He was shot by a drug peddler. It seems he arrested this man some time before. He went to arrest him a second time and they both had a struggle and he shot Jim. As Jim was dead when found, they had only this drug peddler's own confession.
>
> I wonder if you and my brother Jim kept in touch with each other. He was in the police for the past 10 years in Chicago. He never married. He was to come home next year. So when he died he had no near friend but Father Croke from Ballingarry. It was he who took charge of Jim's funeral. He did his best to look up Jim's affairs, but he was taken ill himself and had to go away from Chicago. So we got no account about any of Jim's belongings, only to be informed by the attorney of police that there were 400 pounds in police insurance.

With love from father, Bridie, Jack and myself. I forgot to mention in the letter that mother (RIP) is dead since we heard from you.

(Signed) Stasia Corcoran, Bouleakeale, Kilmanagh, Callan, County Kilkenny, Ireland

572 Bellevue

Early 1914 photo—left couple Uncle Jim and Aunt Edna, right couple my parents

Dad and Mom, Edna and Jim 50 years later

Later we moved to 201 Rosemont Avenue a block away from Drachbar's Bakery, where we could buy gigantic cupcakes for a nickel apiece. Four or five years after that, we moved to 572 Bellevue, right next door to the Jim Dwyers, the family of my father's only sibling and partner in the stationery, magazine and camera shop they started together.

So joined at the hip were the two orphans that throughout their entire lives they took vacations together, socialized together, and purchased adjoining cemetery plots.

Growing up, the Dwyer semidetached houses were just across the street from the Henrys and the Swetnams.

Edward Swetnam was bedridden with tuberculosis and his brother Herbert was an alcoholic. Herbert's wife, Florie, was a Quaker and a former nurse. She had met him while he was a patient in the Trenton State Hospital for treatment of alcohol-related diseases. Herbert was known to us kids for two things: pestering Dad for a bottle of booze and entering the Henry house when, after an evening of tippling, he confused it with his own.

572 Bellevue, equipped with only one bathroom, was eventually the home of nine persons: my sisters Helen, Nan and Del, my brother Ed and me; our parents Nan and Ed; Gran'mom Larkin, her son Albert Larkin (Uncle Al or Unk); and the maid, Mary Moretti.

Helen, Mary Adele (Del), Ann Marie (Nan), Bill, and Ed

Unk was an inspector for the New Jersey Highway Department. His hours were irregular, enabling him to sleep most days as late as noon. He spent just about every night playing poker, often at the Knights of Columbus home downtown.

I recall one night when he lost even the change in his pocket and had to walk home from Morrisville, Pennsylvania, just across the Delaware River from Trenton. I also recall that once, after a long night at the poker table, he arrived at 572 around 6 A.M., just as Gran'mom was setting off for 6 o'clock Mass at Blessed Sacrament Church.

"Ah, Albert," she greeted him. "Up so early. Come along with me. You're just in time for Mass."

"Unk"

Living next door on the other side was the Skokos family: Sidney, Cecilia, Harry, Dorothy, Elaine, Alethea and Jackie, plus their parents. Their father, Peter Skokos, owned the Sugar Bowl Restaurant on North Broad Street in Trenton, and another Sugar Bowl down at the Jersey shore. There was a great to-do one day when the guest of the Skokoses was a visiting Prince of Greece; brother Ed and I, ages eight and ten, respectively, were not particularly impressed. The Skokos kids were polite, well behaved, clean and neat, and good students. Our parents used them often as our role models.

When Mom tried to get us to slow down our garbled speech, she would always say "Speak like Alethea." Ed and I, the older kids of our family, weren't interested in excellence. We had developed other talents: I could whistle, he could wink.

Ed

My first year at nearby Gregory School was my only one in a public school. I remember loving it, especially during a fire drill, when the older boys would come and carry the kindergarteners outside on their shoulders. Thereafter I would be in parochial school, starting in first grade at Blessed Sacrament.

Unk died at the age of 39. A longtime smoker of Murads (a very strong Turkish cigarette), he was afflicted with cancer. He suffered greatly during his last year, which he spent mostly in bed. I remember his moans of pain at 572 and at our summer bungalow at Washington's Crossing. In his final days at the Crossing, it became my job to clean up his midsection several times a day. He had endured extensive surgery at St. Peter's Hospital in New Brunswick, and the stitch holes, dozens of them, leaked blood constantly.

Gran'mom's brother, Monsignor Peter J. Hart

There should have been massive charges for Uncle Al's surgery and aftercare in St. Peter's, but there had been no charges at all. This was because Monsignor Peter J. Hart, pastor of St. Peter's Roman Catholic Church in New Brunswick—as well as Gran'mom's brother and Uncle Al's uncle—was also in charge of St. Peter's Hospital.

Monsignor Hart was treated with great respect on his visits to 572 over the years. He would arrive in the back seat of his chauffeur-driven black Cadillac limousine and preside in the living room for a long hour or more. As the oldest of the five Dwyer children, I would be the first to be summoned to the living room, where in hushed silence Monsignor was comfortably seated, his hands rubbing together, his bald head gleaming.

"Hello, William," he would say (never "Bill") as we shook hands. Then the questions: Was I still an altar boy? What about my spelling, my penmanship, my arithmetic? What did I want to be when I grew up? (He never urged me to consider the priesthood, thank God.)

There was great reverence for the priesthood in our house. We were Irish Catholics. I was to learn that we Catholics were in a club, one that protected its members against other clubs. If you were in a new setting outside that protection, you could find your fellow Catholics by the "code language." In a new school or job, for example, you would casually ask for the nearest Catholic Church, or make a comment about its being Friday—no meat. My father, too close to the days when signs in Philadelphia store windows stated "No Irish Need Apply," wanted that protection and taught us its importance.

The whole family at Helen's confirmation

We obeyed the rules of the church. We ate no meat on Fridays. We said our evening prayers. We attended Mass regularly and went to confession. My father eventually became a trustee of Blessed Sacrament, and when the priest came to our house for Dad to OK the church budget, Father Arthur B. Hayes would carefully conceal the amount with his hand. Dad, a highly respected and successful businessman in town, dutifully signed on the dotted line, never knowing what he actually sanctioned. Message loud and clear: You do not ever question the priest.

The Altar Boy from Trenton, New Jersey

Billy—8th grade

Around this time I learned the Altar Boy Credo:

> That the most important battle of the American Revolution was fought in Trenton, New Jersey, on the day after Christmas in 1776;
>
> That Washington's Crossing, New Jersey, is the greatest summer place in America;
>
> That Gene Tunney, a Marine and a Catholic, is a far better boxer than Jack Dempsey, a Protestant and a slacker in World War I;
>
> That William Shakespeare wasn't a patch on the ass of Joyce Kilmer, whose poem "Trees" is probably the best ever written;
>
> That the United States never lost a war;
>
> That the Roman Catholic Church, established by Jesus Christ and headed by Saint Peter, the first pope, is the only true religion;
>
> That the Pope is infallible in matters regarding religion;
>
> That the New York Yankees, with such Catholics as Babe Ruth, Bill Dickey, and Tony Lazzeri in the lineup, are the greatest team in baseball history;

That the Four Horsemen of Notre Dame were the greatest backfield in football history; and,

That Al Smith, a Catholic, would have been a far better President than Herbert Hoover, a Quaker.

We were not rich but we always had a maid. First, or the first I remember, was a no-nonsense black woman named Octavia (we used "Negro" back in those days, never "black"). She took me on a walk one afternoon when I was three or four years old. I remember climbing the steps with her to the top of the Trenton Reservoir. As we gazed out at the expanse of rippling water, I must have said or done something wrong because Octavia threatened to toss me in the water. She never carried out the threat and certainly meant me no harm. And I never told my parents about it.

Then there was Betty. One afternoon I came home from grammar school to find her sobbing uncontrollably in my mother's arms. "I'm sorry, I'm sorry," she kept saying. She had been caught shoplifting a pair of silk stockings in a downtown store. I remember that my Dad persuaded the owner of the store not to bring charges against Betty and paid for the stockings.

Next there was Edith, who spent much of her time staring out of windows, or reading labels on soup cans, or any cans at all. My clearest memory of her is the time she and the rest of us were listening to the radio broadcast of a football game between Notre Dame and Southern California. At one point Edith made the mistake of saying, "Come on, Southern Cal." Her stay was brief.

Our final maid was Mary Moretti, who remained on the job for six or seven years. When she first arrived, she was about twelve years old. I was about eight and brother Eddie was about six. By the time Mary was fifteen, she was fully developed—short and fat, some would say—and far more sophisticated than we were, especially in matters concerning the birds and bees. On more than one occasion, carefully out of earshot of our parents or in their absence, Mary would read us parts of a ragged little book that she had borrowed from Beatrice, the buxom maid of the Wagners, two doors from our house. I still remember one steamy line that described how "the hairs were intermingling."

I also remember what happened in our cellar one night when our parents were out playing bridge. Ed and I were playing table tennis and Mary was watching. When the game ended, we moved to the pool table. Mary asked if she could join us. We said no. Then she raised the ante: "If I lose, I'll do anything you want me to do, anything at all."

Ed and I looked at each other. Well, why not?

Mary, of course came out third, and Ed and I started a new game without her. But she wasn't through. "So what do you want me to do?" she said. We continued with the game. In silence.

"Well?" she said.

Ed looked up from the table and made a suggestion: "OK, let's see one of your tits."

OK, she'd be right back.

The pool game continued until she returned. Now, instead of a dress, she had on a flimsy crimson terrycloth bathrobe—and apparently nothing else. We stopped the game and looked in her direction.

Well?

Slowly, Mary opened the robe, and—tah dah!—there it was: her right titty out in the open.

It was a big one, all right, but it had no effect on Ed or me, possibly because of the sparse dark hairs and occasional pimple surrounding her nipple. There would be no sin against the Sixth Commandment with regard to ourselves to report next Saturday afternoon at the confessional.

We returned to the pool table and resumed the game.

It was while living at 572 that Ed and I, plus my best friend, Sandy Kerr, got the dream job of distributing weekly circulars touting coming attractions at the Strand Theater on Hermitage Avenue, around the corner from our house. Every Saturday we covered the neighborhood, from Stuyvesant Avenue down to the banks of the Delaware River. We were paid a quarter apiece and were given (wow!) free entry to the theater at any time. So on Saturday afternoons in the 1920s at the Strand Theater we would suffer the interminable wait for Mac, the potbellied organist, who accompanied the silent Westerns we loved. There was joyous applause when he arrived. But he always took time for a pit stop before striding down the aisle to the organ as we yelled our hearts out. After the show we had two choices: a Coke at the Arctic or yesterday's doughnuts (a nickel for a dozen) at Prior's wonderful bakery. Sometimes we could afford both.

It was also during this period that we ran *The Dwyer Press*. Editors: William and Edward Dwyer; weekly contributors: Helen, Nan and Del Dwyer. The first issue came out on January 20, 1933.

We reported such earthshaking events as Gran'mom's finding her glasses, Helen's surprise birthday party, Dad's purchase of a new derby, and Mrs. Fishberg's redecoration of her living room. We also recorded ongoing Checkers and Ping-Pong tournaments and a carefully selected list of Thursday and Friday night's radio programs including *Amos 'n Andy* on WJZ, *Buck Rogers* on WABC, and *The Goldbergs* on WEAF.

It ran two pages and was mimeographed at the store and distributed to our friends, neighbors and family, free. Often at the dinner table I would throw out a question to stimulate the minds of my siblings, always over their groans. If I could get them to think more broadly it would result in better news items for *The Dwyer Press*. For this I was nicknamed the brain of the group, AND because I had submitted a couple of successful questions for "Professor Quiz," a syndicated newspaper column of the time. Some things, however, were too dangerous to print, at least in *The Dwyer Press*.

Forty years later, I wrote about our most dangerous adventure.

And 3 Blackmailing Altar Boys,
The Trenton Times, Sunday Edition, August 8, 1965

It was 1927. Max X was a bootlegger. Everybody knew it. The cop on the beat knew it. The kids on the street knew it. It was one of the facts of life you accepted without question as you grew up in the late Twenties in Trenton, New Jersey.

Herbert Hoover was President. A. Harry Moore was Governor, Frederick W. Donnelly was Mayor.

More importantly, Father Casey was pastor of the Blessed Sacrament parish, and Mother M. Jacoba was principal of the school.

Perhaps even more importantly, Libby Gribbin and Libby Teiss, up on Hoffman Avenue, were the most beautiful girls in the world.

And Max was a bootlegger. That was what was happening.

When Max and his wife rode by in their big black LaSalle, you and the rest of the Smart Alecks on the corner, hands cupped to lips, would yell sing-song style: "Ma-ax is a bootlegger. Ma-ax is a bootlegger." Max would just look at Mrs. Max, one of those "What the hell can you do?" looks, and drive on.

Max lived on Bellevue Avenue, not far from Hermitage. He kept the big LaSalle in a double garage at the rear of his backyard. Behind this garage there was a paved alleyway bordered by a long row of smaller garages. Max used about six of these garages for storage.

On Tick-Tack Night (what we Trentonians called Mischief Night before Halloween) and other nights, you and Sandy K and Bernard C, and maybe a couple of other altar boys, would break into the row garages and carry off some of the evidence. There were boxes and boxes of bottles and crocks piled right up to the ceiling. And fancy red and gold booze labels, thousands and thousands of them. This Max was no small-timer.

He had two regular drivers who kept coming and going all hours of the day and night. Little dark-haired guys. Brothers, everybody said they were Blackie and Little Blackie.

Each brother drove a black Dodge roadster, souped-up and converted. The rumble seat and other stuff had been taken out to make more room for the crates of booze. That's what people said.

The idea of shaking down Max the Bootlegger was born one Saturday afternoon. You and Sandy and Bern rounded up the empty citrate-of-magnesia bottles and turned them in for ten cents apiece at Smith's drugstore at Hermitage and Stuyvesant. There would be enough to get into the Strand Theater and maybe afterwards something left for jelly doughnuts at the Prior Donut Factory.

The movie that Saturday was one of those Warner Brothers epics where a bunch of hoods hurtin' for scratch decide to shake down a gang of bootleggers. Ten grand, they asked for, or else! And they got it. Just like that.

After the movie, as you and Sandy and Bern sat on the curb in front of Prior's eating the jelly doughnuts, somebody came up with the Big Idea: Why not shake down Max the Bootlegger? Huh? Not for ten grand, certainly, but . . . .

In the afternoons that followed, the thing was worked out. You didn't just get together in the schoolyard, or Cadwalader Park or somewhere. You held your meetings after school in the cellar of Sandy's place on Highland Avenue. You and Sandy and Bern sat around a dusty barrel. The only light in the place was that of a candle flickering from the mouth of an old wine bottle. Trying to sound like Warner Brothers gangsters, you made your plans for the Big Caper.

You would write this letter to Max the Bootlegger. A no-nonsense letter that wouldn't sound like a bunch of kids. You'd tell him to come up with twenty dollars—or else!

But where? That was easy. You'd tell him to leave it under that big rock at the corner of Elmhurst and Bellevue, right near the mailbox. There was an empty lot at that corner.

The next thing was—when? When would Max leave the twenty? No problem. Friday night was the only night you could be out as late as 9 o'clock.

Now the letter itself. Sandy's mother had a typewriter. That would be way better than doing the thing in longhand. Edward G. Robinson would never use longhand.

So the letter would be typed. With gloves. No fingerprints or anything. Max would leave twenty under that rock, or else. Bern had a cut on his right elbow so his blood was used to sign the letter with an X. Finally it was finished, and sealed, and stamped, and mailed. The caper was on.
It was a long week. Friday night would never come. Max must have got the letter by now. What would he do? Had it been goofy to ask for just twenty bucks? Why hadn't they gone for more?

Friday night did come. And so, did 8 o'clock. And—"Look, Sandy, it's there!"—the little black Dodge.

As things turned out earlier on that fateful evening, Bern couldn't make it. He had to serve six o'clock Mass the next morning, and his old man had made him go to bed early. So it was just you and Sandy.

Just before 8 P.M. the two of you started out for the corner. The northeast corner of Elmhurst and Bellevue. An empty lot in those days but now there's a fine stone house on the corner, the home of Mr. and Mrs. Thomas J. Foody and family.

Paddling down Elmhurst Avenue toward Bellevue, you and Sandy suddenly stopped. There it was! Not the LaSalle you had somehow expected, but the Dodge. Right there at the corner in the light that reached through the trees. Holy smokes!

What could you do now?

There was no choice but to go on. So you and Sandy went on, striking what you hoped was a natural stride. You got to the corner. As you turned right, you stole a glance inside the car. It was Blackie. Just sitting there, smoking a cigarette and waiting.

You and Sandy kept walking. Up Bellevue to Belmont Circle. To Stuyvesant Avenue. A long, silent pause. What should you do? Down Stuyvesant to Elmhurst. Another pause. What to do? Finally down Elmhurst to Bellevue again.

But it was too late. The little black Dodge was gone. The $20 dream was gone; nothing under that rock.

Gone too was that feeling of guilt that had been eating you all week. All in all it was a great relief. Here at least was one sin you wouldn't have to confess to Father Casey the following Saturday.

But no, come to think of it, you wouldn't have had to confess it anyway. In the final planning stages of the caper, Sandy had made his usual offer. It went like this: If Sandy got $10 of the $20 in blackmail, with you and Bern splitting the other $10, then Sandy would take all of the sin.

Sandy was usually good that way. You and Sandy, say, had glommed three apples from a tree that wasn't yours. You didn't have to worry a minute about the fires of Purgatory or Hell. Not with Sandy there.

"You take one apple," Sandy would say, "I'll take two—and I'll take all the sin."

It was a deal that was hard to beat.

Bill and Ed ages 15 and 13

In our early teens we did some questionable things, such as shoplifting Baby Ruths and other candy bars, but we were "devout Catholics," or at least we thought we were. Brother Ed and I were altar boys proud to assist at 6 A.M. Mass and happy to be serving the Lord. We went to Confession at least once a month.

"Please bless me, Father, for I have sinned." That was how things got under way in the confessional. "I made my last Confession three weeks ago."

First, a tiny one: "I missed my morning prayers about three times." Next a big one: "I had some dirty thoughts about girls, Father." Or, perhaps: "I touched myself improperly." Then back to another safe one: "I missed my evening prayers about three times." And finally: "For these and other sins I ask the absolution of you, Father, please."

That was the planned scenario, but it didn't always work out that way. Sometimes the priest stopped you for details, especially about those dirty thoughts and improper touches.

To avoid such problems we sometimes found it necessary to go downtown and confess at St. Francis Church, better known as the German Church, where the priests were, it was said, more understanding and lenient.

Here I will insert a Catholic joke which seems apropos. One Saturday afternoon this kid's making his confession. He's telling the priest that he's always jerking off, maybe six or seven times a day. The priest, shocked, asks him why, and the kid says, "Because I can't think of anything else to do."

The priest says he wants to have a serious talk with the kid and orders him to go to the rectory and wait for him there. The priest is anxious to get back to the rectory because of what's awaiting him in the kitchen: a juicy cherry pie just baked by the maid.

The kid goes to the rectory and in the kitchen he spies the cherry pie. After a few minutes he decides to have a slice. A little later he has another slice. By the time the priest arrives, the pie's almost gone.

The priest, mad as hell, says, "How could you do such a thing?"

The kid says, "I couldn't think of anything else to do."

And the priest says, "Why didn't you jerk off?"

Around the fifth grade we were finding ourselves the equivalent of today's "cool" when we sang things like "Yank my doodle: it's a dandy." Another ditty we could quote: "Momma's in a whore house, Daddy's in jail, Sister's on the corner yelling 'Pussy for sale!'"

"Do you find it hard getting up in the morning?" we asked a kid who was headed for the priesthood even in fifth grade.

Weather report: "It looked so nice out this morning I decided to leave it out all day."

And the strict teacher's plea: "Just because I made it hard for you, please don't hold it against me."

At 10 years old we thought all this was extraordinarily funny.

Much of the growing-up humor was at the expense of Jews: "Izzy, Ikey, Jakey, Sam. We're the boys that eat no ham. Baseball, football, swimming in the tank. We've got the money but the money's in the bank."

Sad to report, the N word was part of our vocabulary in the early years, both in jokes and even during certain church services. While participating in a procession around the aisles of the church, we altar boys used it in responding to the Latin chanted by the priest. Our response was supposed to be "Liberamus, Domine" ("Free us, Oh Lord"). Instead, we would respond, "Nigger on a stormy day." Adults in the congregation never noticed the difference.

A typical joke: "These two niggers are walking along near a synagogue on Rosh Hashanah. They are startled by a sharp trumpet-like sound.

"'What the hell is that?' one of them asks.

"'They're blowing the shofar,' says the other.

"'My god, they sure know how to treat the help.'"

A significant event occurred when, at age 11 or 12, I decided that on Confirmation Day I would change my middle name. Instead of William Michael Dwyer, I would be William Larkin Dwyer. I didn't even know any Michael in the family, and Larkin was my mother's maiden name. When I told a nun of my planned change, she exploded: "Who ever heard of a saint named Larkin?" and that was the end of it. I don't remember my mother's or father's reaction. But the nun prevailed.

We were sometimes surprised at the way a priest would behave in the confessional. I remember several times when a priest, angered by what had been confessed, shouted to a woman, "I want you to remember that birth control is a serious sin, and abortion is murder!"

Once we noticed a woman kneeling in front of a statue of the Blessed Virgin at a side altar and praying for an unusually long time, sometimes crying.

How come?

We were told she was trying to explain why she was expecting a baby without being married and asking the Blessed Virgin for forgiveness.

Looking back, I find it hard to believe that I remained a Roman Catholic as long as I did. There was no real epiphany, just a slow deterioration in my belief system as the years rolled by—a system that instilled so much fear, so little joy. I remember taking part in a three-day retreat in my freshman or sophomore year at St. Mary's Cathedral in Trenton. It was conducted by a highly touted missionary priest, not by a mere parish priest. The missionary priest's main message had to do with Hell and eternity. He would spend most of one day describing the tortures of Hell: never-ending fire, no hope whatever of escape.

"And you will spend eternity there if you die with a mortal sin on your soul! Just one mortal sin committed before you ask absolution in the confessional!"

The next day the missionary priest spelled out for us just how eternal eternity was: "Imagine that a bird flies more than 500 light years, and you know how long just one light year is, to Betelgeuse, a star in the Orion galaxy. Then the bird picks up a grain of sand and flies another 500 light years back to Earth. The bird returns to Betelgeuse, picks up another grain of sand and flies again to Earth with it. Imagine how long it would take the bird to pick up all of the grains of sand on Betelgeuse and to carry them back to Earth. And, that's only a small part of eternity that never ends."

As we sat in our pews looking up at the priest, I got to wondering, and worrying: What if I committed just one mortal sin—missing Mass, say, on a Sunday—and then was killed in an automobile accident on Saturday morning before I had a chance to have it removed from my soul in the confessional? Would I really spend Eternity in Hell? The answer, of course was yes, and it bothered the hell out of me for a long time.

There were also talks about masturbation: boys going mad, some going blind, losing your ability in athletics as a result. I remember an entry in a diary I kept during the retreat: "Sweet Jesus, keep me pure and clean."

One afternoon during Lent I was saying the Stations of the Cross, as I did every day in that season. About halfway through the stations, I was tapped on the back. It was Father Sullivan, the curate. He asked me to come over to the rectory when I finished. A few minutes later I found myself in the living room of the rectory, seated across from the priest. He got right to the point.

Had I ever thought I might like the life of a priest?

I can't remember my immediate reaction beyond a sputter.

Did I ever think I might have a vocation?

I said I wasn't sure.

Father Sullivan went on for what seemed a long time.

On my way home that afternoon I began to worry about my soul, and where it would end up. Did I have a vocation? Not really, I thought, but I hadn't said that to the priest. Was I turning my back on Jesus? Maybe I did have a vocation.

I remembered that when I was a sixth-grader, about two years earlier, I was almost sure I was headed for the priesthood . . . so was Sandy. We weren't just going to be parish priests; we were going to be missionary priests in China. We were sure of it.

But that resolve had faded. By eighth grade we were thinking of becoming baseball stars or playing football for Notre Dame.

Despite the narrow world I lived in as an Irish Catholic growing up in the 1920s and 30s, our family was as all-American as you could get. We had friends and plenty of food (there was always room for one more at our dinner table), and we were free to roam and explore our tiny world without seatbelts and helmets. Although we weren't wealthy, we lived well and got through the great Depression without much trouble, ending up as members of the Trenton Country Club, a former bastion of WASP reserve.

The part we took for granted, because we were Catholic, was that we kids never doubted our parents would always be there. Divorce was unthinkable.

The Crossing

Nothing was so great as the day Dad and Uncle Jim decided to buy adjoining bungalows overlooking the Delaware River, at Washington's Crossing, New Jersey, so we could have a whole summer vacation while they commuted to and from the store in Trenton. In the blissful summers at Washington's Crossing, my kid brother Ed and I spent the nights inhaling and exhaling fresh air on the screened front porch of our family's bungalow on Washington Avenue, then a dirt lane.

Dad often liked to point out that the bungalow was just as far above sea level as the steeple of St. Mary's Cathedral (in Trenton, eight miles down the Delaware). That was why the air was so good for us.

Our bungalow had four bedrooms, one for my parents, one for Gran'mom and Unk, and the other two divided among my three sisters and any guest they might have. Eddie and I always slept on the front screened porch, through lightning and thunderstorms, protected from rain by big green canvas awnings. It was there we played our many neighborhood card games, which Eddie invariably won. Eddie even then had the easy grace that would be with him his entire life. He was as blonde as I was dark. Because of that his nickname was Pinky. As an altar boy he took the job seriously.

One night on our porch/bedroom, Eddie was kneeling on his cot and saying his evening prayers. There was a light on in a bedroom of the bungalow next door. Our tennis court separated the two bungalows and, on most nights, afforded a clear view of a shapely young woman named Ruth, who was often in the nude. My friend Sandy Kerr and I were preparing for bed on the porch when suddenly he whispered, "Hey, get a load of this." He pointed to Eddie, who was kneeling on his bed, the palms of his hands joined in prayer and farther down in profile, his erect penis.

We swam in the polluted canal (where an occasional dead pig would float by) and in the rock-bottomed Delaware.

Nearly every morning Ed and I exercised the two horses of our next-door neighbor, Clarence "Gilly" Gill, who somehow managed to live like a millionaire on a salary he earned as a driver of a Bell Cleaners delivery truck. Ed's favorite was Red. One of our exercise jaunts involved crossing the bridge to Pennsylvania and riding the horses all the way up the River Road to Lambertville and back, resulting in near destruction of the horses' shoes.

We owned a lot next to our bungalow and found it too small for baseball, our favorite sport. But it was just the right size for a tennis court, my Dad and my Uncle Jim decided. So they hired a farmer, who leveled the ground with the help of a horse and plow. After that, the farmer put up chicken-wire fencing at each end, and we had a tennis court. An Irish conclave, it was busy with Whelans and, too often, visitors from Trenton, as well as Fabers, Nolans, and Dwyers from 9 a.m. until sundown every clear day. Often we played barefoot.

With Dad at the Crossing

There were Sundays when my mother would end up serving dinners of roast beef or chicken to as many as thirty drop-ins. My father soon put an end to that when he manned the grill himself to give my mother a rest from the kitchen, offering hotdogs and summer sausage only, as well as a never-ending supply of ice-cold beer and soda.

Mom, Del and Nan in front of our bungalow

With the rest of the gang, Ed and I occasionally ventured out on foraging missions. The first stop was always the general store near the intersection of the River Road and the road leading to the erector-set bridge over the Delaware River. Ideally, the Old Man would be the only one on duty in the store. One of us would order a five-cent ice cream cone. While the Old Man was slowly getting the cone, and filling the dipper with chocolate ice cream, there was time for us to pocket Tootsie Rolls, Mary Janes, Bolsters and even Tastykakes.

Then we went on to cross the river and strike another target, the Ferry House, the place from which Washington started his Christmas crossing of the Delaware in 1776 before the Battle of Trenton. Along the side of the Ferry House there was a bench topped by a long sign that read: "Come Sit Ye Down and Rest a While." While most of us sat down and rested, one or two would enter a side door to the "refreshment room." The refreshments were nothing but Life Savers, but no one was ever on duty there.

The Rainbow Airport, about a half mile down the river, was on one occasion a part of the tour. First we would say hello to the two men usually on duty at the hangar. Then we would pass on to the lineup of five or six biplanes. As we examined them, one or two of us would head for the refreshment stand at the end of the line. The target there was the locked but easily opened door of a wooden stand open only on weekends.

Carrying our loot, we felt it best not to risk being seen and questioned by the two guys on duty. Instead, we headed downriver to the Yardley Bridge, crossed it back to New Jersey, and headed homeward, a trek that lasted almost three hours.

Back home with our booty, some of us would have conscience trouble: "Aren't we going too far with this? Isn't this a sin, a matter of confession?"

But Jim Faber's brother Bob, a high-school graduate much older and wiser than we were, had a ready explanation.

"It's just a boyish prank," Bob would assure us. "Some day you'll laugh at all this."

One afternoon at Washington's Crossing in the summer of 1933, Jim Faber and I went for a swim in the Canal, which paralleled the Delaware River. The Canal water was not exactly immaculate, but it was only a short walk from our summer bungalows. (To swim in the Delaware, you had to walk all the way over the bridge to the Pennsylvania side.)

Jim and I decided to shed our bathing suits and sneakers so we could enjoy a swim in the nude. (I was always surprised Mom was not upset about this, but she explained that as a farm girl she had never owned a swimsuit.) At one point I decided to head upstream while Jim remained near the flimsy wooden dock. Turning back to the dock, I found my sneaks still there, but my bathing suit was missing.

Hmmm.

Jim thought it might have fallen through one of the holes in the dock. We investigated the dock area and downstream, but there was no bathing suit in sight.

What to do?

Hoping no cars were coming, we clambered up to the River Road—I wearing only my sneaks.

As we pondered the next step, Jim offered to go find something to cover me. OK, but meanwhile what would I do? I couldn't just stand there in the buff; a car was already approaching. I decided to head for the wooded area about a hundred or more yards down the road, and told Jim I'd be waiting for him there.

I set off as the car came closer. The elderly man driving took in the scene but just smiled and passed on. Two other cars slowed down as they approached during my hundred-yard dash, their horns blowing, their passengers hooting and laughing.

My wait in the woods seemed endless, but good old Jim eventually arrived, bearing a set of his own overalls.

Years later, over too many beers, Jim finally made a confession: in addition to saving the day for me, he had been guilty of tossing my suit into the fetid flow of the Canal.

Other bits of summers past:

Accompanying local farmer Hen Crum and his wagon, on Saturday mornings, as he toured the neighborhood selling vegetables from the Crum family's farm;

Swimming in the canal, after finishing our chores, and, as the afternoon train came through, playing "kiss what comes up" as we mooned the astonished passengers;

Cheering the Washington's Crossing baseball team, on a field near the Crum farm in games against such teams as Lambertville, a town north of us, and Fitzgibbon & Crisp, a car dealership from Trenton;

Having a haircut, on a hot and steamy New Jersey afternoon, by a bathing-suited Crossing barber named Elmer, who dove into the canal beneath his shop after completing each shearing;

Listening at night to scary ghost stories told by Horace Clark and Eugene Kelly on vacation from their dental studies at the University of Pennsylvania; they would later become partners in one of Trenton's earliest orthodontic practices; and

Swimming, one lucky summer, in the pool at Somerton Springs, Pennsylvania, a half-hour auto ride away.

The ride was provided by the Hollywood actor Frank Orth, whom we saw years later as the all-knowing bartender in the Doctor Kildare movies starring Lew Ayres. Orth and his wife, son, and daughter had happened upon the Crossing while cruising the area in their Cadillac limo, deciding to spend the rest of the summer as guests nearby in the Washington Hotel. Our families developed a warm relationship, and just about every other night the Hollywood couple would come to play bridge with my parents, the Tom Nolans, "Midge" Fergusons and "Cap" Fabers. They in their vaudeville days had played Trenton several times at The Trent and The Capitol. They had eventually gone on to Hollywood, and they knew all the latest gossip of the 1930s, including the news that Mary Pickford, the wife of Douglas Fairbanks, was running around with Buddy Rogers.

What luck for us! An almost daily ride in the Orth's robin's-egg blue Cadillac limo to the Somerton pool, plus ice cream cones and the ever—popular Tastykakes. It was paradise.

According to age Del, Nan, Helen, Ed and me

The Rich People lived in the stately, red brick mansion situated at the corner of the River Road and a lane without a name. Today the lane, like the other unnamed lanes in Washington's Crossing—which was what we always called our section of Titusville—is paved with macadam and identified by a street sign. It reads Patterson Avenue.

From their large, sloping front lawn, the Rich People could enjoy a sweeping view of the Delaware River and, across the river, a verdant bit of Bucks County, Pennsylvania. On a clear day they could see, even without binoculars, the people swimming on the other side of the river.

The Maddocks, owners of the mansion and a big pottery in Trenton, had an attractive daughter named Cricket. On occasion we glimpsed Cricket arriving or departing in her convertible, long blond tresses swirling in the wind.

One Sunday afternoon back in the late 1920s, the Maddocks and some guests—all in their Sunday finest—were gathered around a game of quoits at the rear of their property. Nearby (on what today is known as Morgan Avenue), five or six of us boys, including my little brother Ed and our cousin Jim Dwyer, were reading the funnies on the front porch of the Nolans' bungalow.

Our curiosity aroused by the clanging quoits, we abandoned the funnies and walked down to take in the action. It was fascinating to be in such company, watching the quoits fly back and forth. Totally absorbed, we apparently failed to notice the Maddocks and their guests were anything but fascinated by our presence. Within a few minutes the game was interrupted by one of the players. He walked over to us, waving a couple of one-dollar bills, and said something like, "Here, you kids. Go get yourselves some ice cream cones."

Wow! In a flash we reached the River Road, turned right and ran past the Log Cabin dance hall, past the Washington Hotel, and reached Kent's General Store, all in less than five minutes. Kent's was next to an Italian delicatessen at the corner of the River Road and the road leading to the bridge over the canal, then to the bridge over the Delaware. In Kent's, we traded the dollars for a monumental feast of ice cream, chocolate Tastykakes, Baby Ruths, creamy root beer, and anything else catching our eyes.

The Golden Age of Tennis

Back in the city of Trenton, tennis was a big sport. Tournament time, in the 1920s and 1930s, was the most serious time of the year. At least it was for the Levys, the Whiteheads, the Waldrons, the Harpers, and a lot of other tennis-addicted families, including the Dwyers. It was a time when you put everything on the line. Either you made a good showing in the city playground department tournaments and gloried in dreams of Wimbledon, or you goofed and then had to wait a whole year to prove you weren't really as bad as all that. Tournament time provided genuine moments of truth for males and females of all ages.

The scene of the annual city championship tournaments was the layout at Cadwalader Park, three long rows of clay courts kept in condition by a crew of workmen headed for many years by a black man named Windom Green. Everybody who was anybody on the local tennis scene turned out for the summer competition. It was conducted under the auspices of the city playground department (headed, as we were frequently reminded, by a man who would appreciate our votes on Election Day: good old George W. Page, Commissioner of Parks and Playgrounds).

Forty or more players signed up for the "midget" competition (for boys up to 14). My cousin Jim Dwyer and I won this championship when we were 14.

Bill and Jim at an earlier date

More than fifty took the courts in the junior boys' division (up to 18), and almost as many competed for the girls' title. And then there were the senior tournaments, with more than 100 players competing in the men's singles championship and fifty or more in the women's tournament. Even more players competed in doubles. Coming out daily or nightly to watch the action were crowds ranging up to and sometimes beyond a thousand. There were times when even Archibald "Spader" Seruby, the Peanut King, who served all the Princeton football games, made the scene, an authentic sign of a major event. This began my lifetime mania for tennis, eventually playing with partners such as Ethel Kennedy, Peter Benchley and John McPhee.

Bill, Ethel Kennedy, Governor Brendan T. Byrne at Morven, the Governor's Mansion at that time

Those were the days when Cadwalader Park was a mecca, especially for boys in their teens, and there were plenty of girls on the scene, too. The Depression was on, people kept saying in the '30s, but none of us seemed to be aware of it. There were penny-ante card games to be played under the shade trees. There were wall-ball games featuring the likes of a future major-league baseball player, George Washington Case, also a good tennis player in those days. There were ice-cold soft drinks waiting at the stand operated by Louis Levy or Jack Brown. And there, out there in the sun, were all those beautiful tennis courts, busy from 9 a.m. to nightfall.

Strangely enough, nowadays, in Trenton, the interest in tennis as a spectator sport is zilch compared to what it was in the '20s and '30s. One reason is that there is no real newspaper coverage of today's tournaments. In bygone days there were banner headlines and full-scale stories about local tennis competition. In later years even a major local tournament was dismissed entirely or kissed off with a drab paragraph or two.

All of which seemed odd indeed to the man who was Mr. Tennis here in the golden age of the sport: Frederick A. (Fritz) Kuser. Throughout the 1920s and 1930s Fritz Kuser was the man to watch in Trenton tennis.

For years the well-kept clay court on the Kuser estate (on Kuser Road) had been a magnet for local tennis addicts including, at times, such national stars as Bill Tilden, Don Budge, Sidney Wood, Frank Shields (Brooke's father), and Althea Gibson.

It was here that Fritz Kuser honed his game in preparation for tournament competition. He proceeded to win the Trenton singles championship twice before 1920 while still in his teens. He went on to win the championship in 1921, 1923, 1925, 1926, 1927, 1928, 1929, 1932, and 1933. Year after year he was the man to beat, and large, enthusiastic crowds kept turning out to see if he could do it one more time.

He finally met his match at Cadwalader Park in the summer of 1934, when he lost in the final round to another legendary figure in local tennis, Bob Boyd. In both 1932 and 1933, Kuser had come from behind to defeat Boyd in the finals. But a year later Boyd came through, and that was Kuser's final season in local singles competition. Boyd won the 1934 match in straight sets and came back to win the title again in 1937.

It was the great play of Kuser and Boyd and such other stars as Leon Levy, Abbie Rednor, Ty Kennedy, Leon Bannon and Eddie Craig that made tennis a big sport here. These were the big names who, as it turned out, helped to instruct and inspire even bigger names in Trenton tennis. The biggest of all, come the 1940s, was Eddie Moylan, the only local player ever to be ranked in the nation's top ten (and who later became the varsity tennis coach at Cornell University). I even wrote a column about him.

My Pick for Trenton's Best Athlete
The Trentonian, August 23, 1977

He took up tennis later in life than most kids who lived in the western section of Trenton. He liked baseball better and he was good at it. But he tried tennis one day at Cadwalader Park when there weren't enough players for a baseball game, and he found it was fun. It was also, he found, far more demanding than fielding and hitting a few baseballs per hour; it was not the "sissy" game that some of the uninformed thought it to be.

And so, Eddie Moylan, at the advanced age of 14, took up tennis. Began to play it every rainless summer day.

There were no indoor courts in those days (except in such unreachable paradises as the Penn Athletic Club in Philadelphia), and therefore when the Cadwalader Park courts were closed in the autumn, the tennis season was over. Most kids put their racquets away until spring.

But not Eddie Moylan. Instead, he found a place where he could practice all by himself in all but the worst winter weather. It was a garage wall a short distance from his home on Edgewood Avenue near Murray Street. Day after day he pounded old balls against the wall, working on his serve and ground strokes.

By the following spring, when the park courts were reopened, Moylan was a much improved player.

He began to beat the kids who'd thumped him the previous summer. And within a short time he was extending that to some of the better players among the men.

A few more summers and he was beating everybody in the Trenton area. And, in Philadelphia, even the celebrated Isadore Bellis. Out in Cleveland, while still in his teens, he made the semifinals of the National Men's Clay Court tournament.

LR Bill, Louis Applestein, Howard Waldron, and Eddie Moylan

World War II interrupted Moylan's rise to the top, but shortly after the war ended he resumed his ascent. While still in the final weeks of service in the U.S. Navy, in late 1945, he won the championship of Ireland, the land of his ancestors.

By the end of the following year, he had developed what such veteran observers as Ellsworth Vines and Allison Danzig were describing as one of the best backcourt games in the world.

This was the year, 1946, when he resumed play in the summer circuit: Rye, Newport, Seabright, and at the end of the summer, the national championships at Forest Hills, Long Island. Along the way he held his own with the best players in the world, including Jack Kramer, Frankie Parker, Ted Schroeder, Tom Brown, Gardner Malloy and Robert Falkenberg. As a result, Moylan made the "first ten" of American players in 1946, No. 9, one below Falkenberg and one ahead of Francisco Segura.

In succeeding years Moylan improved so much that in one season of tournaments he extended Jack Kramer, the world champion, to three matches of five sets each and defeated Kramer once.

Moylan moved up to No. 8 in the national rankings for 1947. The next year he was still in the top ten with a No. 9 ranking.
In the late 1950s he achieved the dream of millions of young players by making the U.S. Davis Cup team. In football the equivalent would be All-American. In baseball the All-Star team.

Competing against such players as Victor Seixas, Tony Trabert and Hamilton Richardson, Moylan did so well in 1954 that the U. S. Lawn Tennis Association people ranked him seventh in the country. The next year he moved into fifth, and in 1956 was No. 4 in America, highest ranking of his career.

Of the scores of skilled players trying to make it on the national tennis circuit, only three, Richardson, Seixas, and Herbie Flam, were rated ahead of him.

Moylan went on to become chief tennis professional at some of the world's most prestigious centers, including the West Side Tennis Club at Forest Hills.

He is now [1977] coaching the tennis and other racquet teams at Cornell.

In making the Davis Cup team, and in reaching the top ten of American tennis for six years, Eddie Moylan proved himself to be, in my opinion, not only the best tennis player to come out of Trenton but also the athlete most skilled at his sport. Translate that No. 4 national ranking achieved by Moylan in 1956 into some other sports and you have some idea of how great his achievement was. Imagine the Trenton area producing the fourth-best baseball, football or basketball player in the USA. Not just in a certain weight class as, for example, in boxing, but in the entire competition. There would be no end to the local celebrity of such an athlete.

Well, Eddie Moylan, the kid who used to pound 'em against that garage wall behind Edgewood Avenue, deserves such celebrity. And he's my nomination for the best athlete ever to come out of the Trenton area.

College Days

Mother was probably right in her contention that my "loss of faith" began at Trenton State Teachers College in 1935 and 1936, my freshman and sophomore years. (Good friends of Mom and Dad said the same thing had happened to their daughter at Trenton State. They, like the Dwyers, felt guilty about it.)

After two years at Trenton State Teachers College (now The College of New Jersey)—two of the happiest years of my life—I transferred to Saint Joseph's College (now University) in Philadelphia. At Trenton State the ratio was something like 10 girls to every boy because in those days, probably due in part to the poor pay, the teaching field was dominated by women, except for physical education, which attracted some guys and types like me still looking for a groove. My mother had encouraged me to be a teacher and was the one who urged me to take the entrance exam. Also it was the Depression and the price was right. If memory serves me, the yearly tuition was something like $175.

Mostly the male/female imbalance was great, except for one spring afternoon in 1935. The teacher was chalking instructions of some kind on the blackboard, making the only sound in the room. There were about 25 of us in the class, all but five or six female. Seated near the back of the room, along with the male majority, I was on the verge of falling asleep.

As a result, I almost jumped out of my seat when a friend who shall remain nameless, seated behind me, expelled a tremendous blast of intestinal gas.

As I turned toward him, I was surprised—stunned—to hear my friend John Gardner, seated at my left, shout, "Dwyer, you dirty dog!"

Oh, no, I thought, they'll think it was me! I could feel myself starting to blush. The girls' faces were all turned to me, and so was the teacher's.

My denials proved to be unavailing, and for what seemed an endless time I was known as the Guy That Let the Big One in Math Class.

That really wasn't the reason I transferred out of Trenton State. I made the change because I decided to be a journalist, perhaps even a writer, and not a teacher as my mother had hoped. Under the Jesuits at St. Joe's, the journalism program consisted of logic and epistemology and many other "philosophy" subjects, lots of English, and weekly talks by Leo Riordan, a reporter for the *Philadelphia Inquirer*. The course was not exactly on a par with The Columbia School of Journalism.

It is not a complete exaggeration to say that in philosophy classes most of our time was spent learning that Kant, Nietzsche, and Marx were wrong, and Roman Catholic philosophers like Thomas Aquinas were right about everything.

While studying journalism at Saint Joe's, I worked as campus correspondent for the *Philadelphia Bulletin* and on many afternoons covered high school sporting events as well. The pay was fairly good—as much at $5 for covering a football or baseball game. By phoning in the final score to a local news service called Scholastic Sports, I was able to make myself a cool 50 cents extra. That $5.50, by the way, was enough to buy dinner for two weeks at the Golden Arrow Diner, on City Line Avenue across from the college. At that diner we once witnessed the owner serve a platter to a uniformed black chauffeur in silence, then pick up a shaker and cover his entire dinner with salt. Before the driver quietly got up and left, he bowed his head and wept. It was a short lesson I would never forget.

On the afternoon I remember best, I ventured out to cover a track meet involving several high school teams. An accident tied up traffic and I was a couple of hours late, and I was due to make my first call to the *Bulletin's* sports department within a few minutes. What to do? I looked around for meet officials, and for the guys who usually covered for the *Ledger, Inquirer* and *Record,* but in vain. Finally, and I forget just how it came about—perhaps because I looked so frantic—a man in an overcoat with a turned-up collar accosted me and asked if I was looking for the results, so far, of the track meet. Yes, I said, greatly relieved. Thereupon the man shook my hand, introduced himself as "Red Smith of the *Record*," took a notebook out of his overcoat pocket and proceeded to save my life, giving me the win-place-and-show of the 100-yard-dash, the half-mile, the 440-yard relay, and so forth. I was not only relieved but also flabbergasted. At that time Red Smith was already a big name in Philadelphia, and his stuff was so good that you knew he would be a big name nationally some day. Thanks to him I made my deadline.

From time to time as the years went by, I thought of taking the time to send him a belated note of thanks. And then I picked up the paper one day to learn that Pulitzer Prize sports columnist Red Smith had died.

If I did believe in sin, I'd say that procrastination ought to be one of the cardinal sins.

The Newspaper Business

I came by sports writing naturally perhaps. I was a tennis player, having perfected my game over countless summers on our homemade tennis court at The Crossing. I won the Trenton singles championship at Cadwalader Park when I was 14, and at 18 I was junior champion. At Trenton State, and at St. Joe's, I was captain of the tennis team. My sisters all played tennis.

*Trenton State College Tennis team,
I am 3rd from right in front row*

My kid brother Eddie followed me to St. Joe's and became captain of the golf team. It was great having him there but not unusual, since he was always one step behind me all our lives. Because of his effortless charm and luck at most of his endeavors, he made many friends. And he was such a decent guy. He never talked about his prowess with girls, which was considerable. And on more than one occasion, one of my sisters back home would have a friend who needed a date for a prom. Invariably, she would make a desperate appeal to Eddie and of course he would comply. No big deal. Not to mention the girl would feel euphoric with a good-looking college boy as her date.

It was at St. Joe's that I learned another life-changing lesson. When I was a senior something devastating happened to me.

I had a seizure.

I had been sitting in a classroom with about twenty other students when it hit me—a sort of buzz, followed by a dizzy feeling, then out. I came to an hour later, lying supine on the carpet in the office of the college president. At first I had no idea where I was. The first thing I noticed was that my shoes had been removed, revealing a big-toe hole in my socks. My shirt collar and tie had been loosened.

They told me I had slumped unconscious at my desk, and that was about all they could say. I remembered feeling dizzy in class, that my head started spinning out of control, but nothing more. I felt all right, except for a slightly sore tongue. I learned I had bitten it in a couple of places. Mostly, I felt embarrassed about the hole in the sock.

Later in that school year, a month or two before graduation, I had two more seizures, each preceded by what I came to know as an aura: a sort of buzzing accompanied by dizziness just before losing consciousness. I said nothing about this to my parents, but somehow they learned about them, and on my next visit home I found they had arranged a visit to the doctor. The doctor checked my pulse and my blood pressure, asked a lot of questions: diet, bowels, state of mind. Was I worried about anything at college? About the future?

I couldn't give him any answers, but, years later, I came to believe that worries about my future really were related to the seizures. The Great Depression was still on. My father had worked hard at the family business and hoped I would join it. But my heart wasn't in the family business. I was interested in becoming a writer, or at least a journalist. I had worked part-time for three summers at the *Trenton Times*. During the school months I had enjoyed covering sports for the *Bulletin*.

St. Joe's graduate

After graduating, I purposely chose journalism over the family business, with the hope of some day attaining a fraction of the success Red Smith achieved.

In the summer of 1939, following graduation, I started looking for a job. Here and there, on a sticker pasted on the rear window of an automobile was the question: "Wasn't the Depression Terrible?" But the Great Depression of the 1930s was still on, and jobs were hard to come by. Especially in the newspaper business.

I made the rounds of newspaper offices in Philadelphia, New York and elsewhere. I filled out job applications until my fingers were numb. But no paper was hiring anybody except an occasional copy boy at something like $12 a week.

The Bulletin seemed like a good possibility since I'd already worked for that paper part-time as a stringer while attending St. Joe's. And the city editor there, Larry Flick, was the father of a tennis partner of mine at college. Maybe there was a chance.

Fat chance! More than 50 college graduates, Flick told me in tones as gentle as possible, were competing for the next copy boy job, one that might come up in a few months. Or might not. The latest copy boy hired by the *Bulletin*, at $15 a week, was a graduate of the U. S. Military Academy.

I had, of course, already tried the *Trenton Times* newspapers, but they hadn't hired a new reporter in years. The only possibility there was to become a stringer for the sports department—to cover events that staffers didn't want or have time to cover, at so much per newspaper column inch. So I did it! I covered golf tournaments, dart matches, bowling—anything—and for my efforts received $3 a column, a column being 22 inches of news considered fit to print, no headlines included.

Each day I clipped my stuff from the *State Gazette* and the *Evening Times* and pasted the articles together in a single column roll. By the end of a good month the roll would be big enough to choke a horse. I would take it in to Russ Thomas, then sports editor of the *Times*, and Bill O'Donnell, sports editor for the *Gazette*. I eventually received something like $100 for the month's work.

My days as a stringer came to an end one summery Saturday, when I spent something like 12 hours at George Schick's typewriter in the old Times building on Stockton Street. George covered the State House Monday through Friday, and his desk was available to the sports department on Saturdays.

I came in around 9 a.m. that Saturday and started hacking away at a pile of stuff Russ Thomas had left to be rewritten—scrawled notes on quoits tournaments, box scores of baseball games in the nearby small towns of Hightstown and Titusville, girls' hockey results, stuff like that. I stretched out each item as far as possible, and by noon I figured I'd written the equivalent of four or five 22-inch columns. Not bad.

Then Russ came in with more work. And kids kept bringing in results of track meets, swimming meets, tennis matches.

I kept grinding out copy right up to the Saturday night deadline, pausing only for a ham on rye or two. Then it was time for a beer or two at Tony Kall's emporium, and on to bed.

The next day I had to buy an extra copy of the *Sunday Times Advertiser*. My stuff was on both sides of most of the sports pages. I clipped out every line I'd written. I pasted it all into a long roll. I measured the roll against the 22-inch column length and discovered that in one day I had written 17 columns—374 inches of copy. That translated into $51!

Such affluence was not to last. A short time later, the *Trenton Times* newspapers put me on the payroll as a full-time general assignment reporter. At $25 a week. No more $51 Saturdays, but at least the job was steady. I guess it wasn't so bad. My cousin Jim Dwyer, fresh out of Villanova, was working as a teller at a bank called the Trenton Trust five days a week plus Saturday mornings for a grand total of $50—a month, that is.

On the job in the Trenton Times newsroom

For about four years I wrote everything from obituaries to feature articles. Some unbylined stories involved interviewing members of the large Chambersburg family of a nurse who, along with her boss, had died in the nude in the back seat of a car, having left the motor on to keep warm; celebrating the 100th birthday of a female resident of a Burlington Rest Home whose every answer to my many questions was accompanied by a thunderous blast of intestinal disturbance; covering a soapbox derby in Ohio with some local participants; and fracturing a rib or two while the wrestler Maurice Tillett, known as "French Angel," demonstrated his famous bear hug on me at the Trenton Armory.

Tony Kall's saloon on Front Street was the favorite gathering place for *Times* reporters in those days and for decades to come. It was a handy place for lunch and evenings as well. Tony was a good host, but there were times when he ran out of patience with unruly customers and those he just didn't like. I remember a night when a guy came in and Tony refused to serve him. "You're serving everybody else," he said, "why not me?" Tony looked him straight in the eye and said, "Because you're a pain in the ass." The guy just said, "Oh." And, while the others looked on, he walked out of the place, never to return.

It was a sweet time. I was living at home on the cheap and excited about working in my chosen field. The future looked bright.

Then the war came.

PART II

The War

On Sunday afternoon, December 7, 1941, news of the Japanese attack on Pearl Harbor reached President Franklin Delano Roosevelt. Minutes later, that news shocked the whole nation. A week later *The Nation* reported on the scene in Washington:

Within an hour the radio had it, and the streets were clogged with government workers, high and low, on the way to offices where there was nothing for most of them to do.

Crowds that gathered around the White House behaved like none the capital had ever before seen. People just stood and looked. They seemed to be ready for bombs or a circus parade, and eager for either. They wanted to do something but didn't know what. Finally they sang *God Bless America*.

Glamour Boy Aviator

Ed (extreme left) with pals in flight training school

Ed went first. Right out of college. He was nuts about airplanes, so it was not surprising that he signed up as a cadet for the Army Air Corps on January 5, 1942, training at Maxwell Field, Alabama, and receiving his wings on September 6, 1942 at Turner Field, Georgia. He was the glamour boy aviator while I was designated 4-F because of the seizures. I didn't feel terrific about that.

Pretty soon we were getting letters home describing his flight training.

November 10, 1942

Dear Folks,

It looks like things are at last getting started. We checked everything today and will leave 5 o'clock tomorrow morning, Wednesday.

My PO # is different and so is my trip. We're not going to fly as previously scheduled but we will fly cargos and personnel from Accra, Africa, to other parts of Africa. We'll be over there for about 45 days and then we should get back to Washington. It's a special mission and almost our whole outfit from Washington is going. So it's going to be a great trip and I'll tell you all about it when I get back. We're flying the same airplanes as we were before. It's the C-87 (converted B-24).

I probably won't be very punctual with my mail so just remember that no news is good news. We'll be kept moving most of the time and I probably won't be near the incoming mail but don't let this stop you because I'll be getting it some time. I'll write as often as I can and won't be able to say much because of the censors, so don't think I'm trying to baffle you.

Please, Annie (mother) don't worry about me because I'm in the best of health, will be under the best care and I have been to confession and communion here. So everything is in the hands of God.

It's not a dangerous journey and is one that will give me about the best flying experience you could ever hope for.

Well, Sweethearts, this is about all I know for the present. I hope everyone is well and that Willie gets in some branch of the service he likes.

So long for now,

> As ever, all my love to all.
> Ed

P.S. I'll be thinking about you all, all the time.

November 16, 1942, Sunday, 10 o'clock

Dear Folks,

Arrived here Friday the 13th. It was a great trip and everything went along fine. We left Florida

Wednesday morning at about 7:30 A.M. and just kept on a going. We made a few stops on the way. All in all the trip was 7,000 miles. It took 55 hours from the time we left Fla. until we landed here. We had two shifts and took turns sleeping.

The country here (in Africa) is very interesting and our Post is exceptionally good. The food is much better than I had expected and the beds are even better than those we had in the States. The weather is great, a good breeze all the time. The beach here is just like that at Stone Harbor (New Jersey) and the water is grand.

The natives wait on tables and clean your rooms and make the beds, drive the buses and cars around and do mostly everything. They're very funny and can talk English—almost—so it's great trying to tell or ask them something.

Mass was at 8:30 and was held here at the Post. Boy, it was nice to see the crowd that attended. The Chaplain is a missionary who was brought in by the Army. He gave a nice talk and seems to be quite an interesting man.

We're having a meeting this afternoon so it looks like we'll start working tomorrow. I won't be able to write anything about the trips but I'll tell you all about them when I get home. We're not supposed to be here long and there's a chance of being home around Christmas or New Years. So, Pop, you'll have to wait until I see you before you can tell the boys at the Hildebrecht (hotel in downtown Trenton where his father often had lunch) what I'm doing.

It's a funny thing down here. All the boys, or at least half, grow mustaches and goatees. So at present I'm growing a third eyebrow. There's not much to it at present but I'll keep you posted on its progress.

Here on the Post we have a movie about four times a week and they're going to have them every night soon. We also have nice recreation rooms and also the lovely beach. So we have it pretty nice when we're not flying. And the best thing about the outfit is the men in it. I'd say there are about 60 of us all told, and they're all about the best men you could find anywhere. It's just like one big happy family.

All my love,
Ed

November 27, 1942, Africa

Dear Folks,

Thanksgiving has come and gone here and mine was the most unusual I ever spent. Believe it or not we had turkey with all the trimmings and even had pumpkin pie. I can guess that yours was a bit better than ours, but we all consider ourselves very lucky in that we had it too. The food here is still remarkably fine and I still have two chop-chop every night. That means two platters.

Another amazing thing happened and that is yesterday was the first day I ever went swimming on Thanksgiving. I know before we always used to freeze out at the Trenton High game. But this year I spent mine basking in the sun. Boy, when this war is over I at least shall have improved my swimming.

Today makes two weeks that we've rested and at present I'm in top form. Some of us should go out next week so if I'm lucky maybe I'll get in a little flying before I return. We're still here for no more than 45 days and for that reason we're only used when they have no one else. They figure there's no sense in training us when we're going to leave in a short time.

I have a lot to be thankful for and consider myself very fortunate to be with this Command. I could have very easily been sent to combat and at times wish I were when I think of all the good boys who are fighting. But since fate has been so kind, I'll accept her kindness.

Here's hoping you're all in fine shape. As yet I haven't received any of your letters but expect them in a day or two. I do hope you're receiving mine.

So long for now.

As ever, all my love to all,
Ed

Dec. 6, 1942

Dear Folks,

Received Mother's letter yesterday and was a bit startled. But when I noticed the post mark, November 19th, it all cleared up. It's the first I've received from home.

Originally we were to fly the shuttle but that was changed and instead of being in South Africa we're stationed in Africa where the shuttle we were supposed to fly lands. And from here we fly all over. I can't say where.

Last Wednesday I made my first trip and we got back here Saturday. It was great and I saw quite a bit more of the country. I saw the Mediterranean and it looked pretty good and I may have gained a pound or two. The water is still wonderful and my swimming is oh ki doke.

Mother's letter makes me believe she's worrying about me, but I'll presume now that you have received my other letters she's the same "Annie" again.

We're still uncertain about coming home and should know something in a week or so. It sure would be nice to be home for Christmas. As soon as I know anything definite I'll let you know.

I'm rooming with Goedeke, the lad from Maryland. We each have a good single bed, closet, bureau and desk. There is a shower and toilet for every two rooms. The mess hall is only a few doors away and this we visit quite frequently. So Dearies everything is Jake here in Africa.

As always all my love to all,
Ed

December 14, 1942

Dear Folks,

You'll have to excuse the paper because this is all that's available and about all that could be had within a radius of 1,000 miles. At present I'm somewhere in the middle (flying over the middle) of a great big desert. We're going a little better than 200 miles per hour and are at 8,000 ft. The sun is out and shining for all it is worth. There's a bit of a haze from the sand but it's not too bad. The surrounding terrain is un-picturesque. It is all sand with a few sand hills thrown in every now and then.

This is my second trip and it was the same as the first. We've been in the air now for about seven hours and won't land for at least another three. But you get used to it and the time passes rather fast. We have good radios and get music every now and then. We also had food and water aboard and there's a lot to be done.

I'm writing this in the Navigator's desk and I hope you can read it because as the plane moves so does the desk.

Well Dearies, I've been receiving your letters and Mother's tone has changed 100% from that of her first letter. I'll close now and add more when we get to our African home.

Well, we landed home at around 5 o'clock. Had a good supper and hit the hay.

Today is Monday the 14th and 'tis beautiful as are all the days down here. I believe we've only had about 1 hour of rain the whole time I've been here.

Still uncertain about coming home. I'm quite sure we can't make it by Christmas and I can't say if we do get home it'll be the first week in January. I suppose everybody at home is getting ready for Christmas and are in the old Christmas spirit. Down here it doesn't seem much like Christmas. It's more like the fourth of July. The only time we hear anything about Christmas is in church on Sunday.

This piece of paper is not supposed to be a clue to where I've been; it's merely a piece of borrowed paper (Heliopolis House Hotel, Cairo).

I'll close now and bid you a Merry Christmas. Please don't feel sorry for me because I'm not home because there are a lot more places where I could be that could be a lot worse and I've also seen a few of these places. In fact I haven't seen a place that can touch it here.

All my love to all,
Ed

December 22, 1942

Dear Folks,

By the time you receive this Christmas will have come and gone and I hope you all had a nice white one.

I just got back from another trip up to North Africa and as usual it was OK. It's a bit colder up that away and it's sure great to get back to the land of sunshine. One night you sleep with four blankets and the next night you only need a sheet. But I'm still as healthy as ever and these quick changes in climate haven't bothered me in the least. But then again we have good equipment and are always dressed according to the weather.

Received Del's letter and was glad to hear that she and the gals are having a good time. It takes us about 10 days to get a letter but no matter how long it sure is good to hear from home. I suppose Del thinks she's quite the kid, now that she's had a weekend in New York.

I'm sorry I wasn't home to get a gander at Mother and Aunt Edna working in the store. (They helped during the Christmas rush.) I suppose the Dwyer brothers had one of their best Christmases yet at the store and I'll bet the Mother Dwyers will say it was because of them that business was so good. I sent a few Christmas cards and hope they all reach Trenton somewhere in the neighborhood of Christmas.

Oh—before I forget it, Goedeke and I bought a camera from one of the boys here and films are impossible to get in this country so, if you can, please send me a few rolls of size 127. I don't know if the camera's any good, and we won't until we get some of the rolls developed. We've taken about four rolls and have two left. So if you can, please send us some.

As yet we haven't heard anything about coming home and we also haven't heard anything about staying. So our chances are still about 50-50.

So long for now,
Ed

December 28, 1942

Dear Folks,

Christmas has come and gone here and it was just a bit different than I had expected. To be sure I spent half of Christmas at about 10,000 feet in the air. I had a trip up north that started at 11:30 Christmas Eve. So I didn't even get to church. We flew for about 11½ hours and spent the remainder of the day trudging through the North Africa mud. Went to bed early and left the next day for home.

They still had the Christmas dinner menu up here and boy it looked plenty good. Our Christmas dinner was Spam and hot raisins. But I'm not kicking because the boys up there are doing a good job and are really roughing it.

Our 45-day temporary duty ended on the 27th and as yet we're not sure if we're to stay or go back to the States. There are lots of rumors floating around here as to what we're to do, and the ones that seem the most logical are that we're to get a 60-day extension of orders and that we'll probably move up North and fly a route that will take us to the land across from where (censored) is. But whatever comes up will be OK by me because it sure would be great to get home, and then if I stay here I'll get about the best flying experience you could ever ask for. So I can't lose no matter what happens.

Last week we all took a short sight-seeing tour through the jungles. We covered about 170 miles. The scenery was beautiful and the jungle was something to see. We went through quite a few of the native villages and the natives got as big a kick out of us as we did out of them. Here's hoping you're still in fine shape and that you had a good start for the New Year.

So long for now, as always, all my love to all,
Ed

January 5, 1943

Dear Folks,

As I believe I've told you, I expected to be moved up to North Africa. Well, that's exactly where I am now. We're supposed to be here for about two months and probably won't be home until April.

*Ed with some natives in Marrakech,
French Morocco, January 1943*

The town here is really something and the natives are French and Arabic. The town is beautiful and we're staying in a big hotel. As usual our time is free except when we fly and this gives us a chance to see the sights. The town is bounded on almost all sides by big mountains and some are about 15,000 ft. high. They're always covered with snow and make quite a picture. We can look up from the city and see these mountains with the snow on them and be standing right next to a row of orange trees covered with big beautiful oranges.

The mail situation up here is quite bad and I don't think I'll catch up with mine for a couple of weeks; but keep writing because I'll get them some day. My letters will slow down a bit because it's hard to get them mailed, and the only way we can do this is to catch a plane going south and hope the pilot will mail them for us. Otherwise they'd do it by boat. So once again I say that no news is good news.

Hoping to see you in April.

All my love to all,
Ed

January 13, 1943

Dear Nannie (sister),

Received your letter dated Dec. 31 yesterday and the thickness of the envelope told me what was in it before I opened it. It also made me happy when your written word confirmed it. My only regret is that I wasn't home New Year's to congratulate you. So I'll take the time now to offer you and Ed

[Schmierer] my best wishes and every hope for your future happiness.

It didn't surprise me because as I've said I rather expected it. I know you picked a good man and know that I firmly believe you've done the right thing because it'll give you both something to hang on to while Ed's away.

So Nannie Dear, you don't have to make excuses to me. Just be proud of what you're doing. I suppose it was quite an ordeal trying to tell the Folks, but if they had objections they'd have told you a lot sooner than now. All they're trying to do is make sure that you're sure of what you're doing.

I'll bet Bill, Helen and Del sort of gave you a good kidding, but don't worry about them because they're all right there rooting for you.

Where we go next is hard to say, but wherever it is it'll be interesting and the fact that we're always moving around gives us plenty to look forward to.

All my love,
Ed

January 13, 1943
Postmarked Miami, Fla.
(they could never give exact locations]

Dear Folks,

Received Mother's letter of the 3rd this morning.

We had a marvelous time up North and stayed at the resort city of Accra, North Africa. We lived in a hotel all the time and had a life of leisure for about eight days.

Man, we were learning how to talk French and if we'd stayed longer I think we'd all been able to get along. Our food was great and we had good wine with every meal. We used to eat dinner at 1, have coffee and toast at 5, and supper at 8.

In the city itself it was and is unbelievable to see how the Arabs live. Their homes are down dark dingy alleys and are dirty and very poorly ventilated. They have no heat and no lighting facilities, but the French homes are beautiful and very well kept up. There are very few cars in the city and the majority of people ride around on bicycles. All the taxis are horse-drawn carriages and it was fun riding in them.

On Sunday Keegan and I went to mass at the French church. It was very pretty and had its school alongside. The mass was the same but the people seemed to do as they pleased; some kneeling, others standing or sitting. At first we tried to follow them but it was impossible so we did what we all do back in the States. It was a High Mass and the singing was beautiful.

As usual the people took a great liking to the Americans. They haven't had sweets up here for a few years and all of us would give them candy and chewing gum. They're especially fond of gum and everywhere you go the children ask you for some.

So long for now, all my love,
Ed

Helen, Nan, Del and me before I joined up

Back home in 1943 with the help of a doctor who was a friend of the family, I got my classification changed to 1-A, and went into the Army. Why? Partly I was bored with life as an unmarried civilian, especially a 4-F civilian. Or maybe I was afraid I was missing out on a once-in-a-lifetime opportunity. It was anything but a matter of patriotism. Perhaps it was mostly a matter of catching up with my little brother Eddie, two years younger than I, and already a pilot flying supplies from India to China for the troops of Chiang Kai-shek. When he came home on leave, I envied him and the silver wings he had earned. We had been together all of our lives and I missed him. It was not a time for me to be a civilian—not a time to be inside while all the rest of the boys were out on the playing field.

Among the last things I remember about 572 Bellevue Avenue was the beautiful spring morning that year when I left the house and walked to Gregory Elementary School. There I joined a group of draftees who were to be inducted at Fort Dix that day into the Army. I later learned that, shortly after I left the house, Gran'mom said, "I'm never going to see Bill again."

Her prediction was right: she died from a stroke before I ever saw home again.

I Become a Spy

Private Dwyer

During the summer I had completed seventeen weeks of basic training at Camp Wheeler, about four miles from Macon, Georgia. Several weeks included training as a member of an Intelligence and Reconnaissance platoon to substitute for an I&R man killed or wounded in combat. We learned to gather information about enemy positions and plans and to go on patrols—sometimes at night behind enemy lines to reconnoiter the enemy.

One afternoon I was sitting in a pecan grove with the rest of the platoon. Each of us had an M1 at hand, and an officer was leading us through the process of disassembly. I had never before even had a gun in my hands. After several attempts I managed that afternoon to disassemble then reassemble my rifle. At one point I almost lost an eye.

The days in Georgia were long. For one thing, the natives were not happy to see us. One day, a platoon-mate returned to report a sign on the front door of a Macon eatery that read, "No Dogs or Enlisted Men Allowed." We sort of evened things by marching along the sandy road and chanting, "Georgia is a hell of a state, the asshole of the forty-eight."

There were about fifty members of the platoon, almost all college graduates, and all of them friendly, or at least not contentious. All of them, that is, except Ollie Goldsmith, "that son of a bitch," as he came to be known. Early in the training, Goldsmith, a native of Chicago, managed to get himself detested by just about every other member of the platoon. There were times when he seemed to be determined to take on the whole bunch. "You're nothing but a bunch of suckers, all of you," he was fond of saying while we were "taking ten" during a march or while waiting in a chow line. According to Goldsmith, the damned war was not started by the Japanese at Pearl Harbor but by President Roosevelt—an idea unthinkable at the time. The whole business was a fraud, he said, and only a sucker would take it seriously.

Only a "thucka" would. That was how Goldsmith put it, afflicted with a pronounced lisp and thus unable to handle such a word as "sucker." As the weeks wore on, he made it clear to anyone within hearing distance that, by God, he wasn't going to go overseas like the rest of the "thuckath." He was going to be right here in the USA, safe and sound, while the rest of us were getting our asses shot off overseas. He would piss on our graves, or, as he put it, "pith on our gwaveth." His father was not only CEO of a major corporation but also a personal friend of the famous General X. So he claimed. "And while the reth of you thucketh are getting your atheth thot off," Ollie said, he'd be sitting out the war in Washington, DC. "And not as a goddam private, either."

Ollie was frequently challenged to fights, but he managed to talk his way out of it; he just "couldn't be bothered." Except for one day we all knew would come. The challenge came from Johnson, a compact and muscular guy from North Carolina. Ollie had, not so accidentally, bumped into Johnson in the mess hall that morning, and the fight had almost started right there. But Sergeant O'Hara stepped in between them and ordered them to postpone the fisticuffs until after dinner that evening.

Goldsmith was at last going to get the beating he deserved. That afternoon, at the rifle range, we couldn't wait for fight time to arrive. When it did, we formed a square outside the barracks and the fight began. Both were wearing plump boxing gloves. Sergeant O'Hara was the referee, and somebody was timing the three-minute rounds.

By the end of round one it appeared that Johnson, swinging ferociously, was more powerful than Goldsmith. But Goldsmith had far longer arms and knew how to take advantage of his reach. By the end of round two, it was clear that Goldsmith was by far the better boxer. By the middle of round four, Johnson was staggering and his face was a bloody mess.

Sergeant O'Hara stepped between them before the round ended and declared the fight over. In muttering silence, we returned to the barracks.

About halfway through the training, I was handed an opportunity to even the score with Goldsmith. On a Sunday afternoon I was summoned, by way of the squawk box in our barracks, to the orderly room. There I reported to a lieutenant who explained that I had been selected for a special assignment. Ah! A job with *Stars & Stripes*, or perhaps with *Yank*? No such luck. Once a week I was to report any "subversive" statement or "suspicious" behavior on the part of any member of the platoon.

Wow! I was thinking of Goldsmith as I returned to the barracks. Following instructions, each week thereafter I mailed a letter to the nonexistent "Bibb Photo Company," as if I were an employee of that company on vacation. "Dear Gang," I opened each letter, and proceeded to report the latest possibly subversive behavior of Private Ollie Goldsmith. Toward the end of the training, there wasn't much to report except a phrase he'd been using almost daily: "I'll pith on your gwaveth."

Somehow—I don't remember how—I eventually learned that there were at least two other spies in the platoon—older guys like me. Both of them had been reporting week after week the same things I had been reporting. Maybe, we agreed, Goldsmith wouldn't be pissing on our graves, after all.

When basic training was over, Goldsmith was among the first to leave camp for further assignment. We hoped it would be for combat, but we weren't really expecting it. Each day for about two weeks, five or six platoon members departed, some for Europe and some for the Pacific. Finally five or six guys were left, including me. With no duties to perform, we spent much of our time playing poker and wondering where the hell we would end up.

One afternoon I woke up on a cot in an aid station not far from the barracks. At first I didn't know where I was or how I got there. Then I remembered. I had been playing poker. Oh, God, I thought, had I had another spell? Had this been another aura—a dizzy feeling I vaguely remembered? If so, it was the first since my senior year in college. I looked around the aid station. A corporal was seated at a table nearby. What to do? After some thought, I decided to bluff my way out. Pretending to just have awakened, I stretched my arms, gave an exaggerated yawn, and started to get up from the cot.

"Guess I'll get on back to the barracks," I said as casually as I could.

"Oh, no, you don't," the corporal said. "You stay right where you are. Captain wants to talk to you."

It was up to me. That was the upshot of my talk with the captain, a doctor. Did I want to go home, or stay in the Army? This was my fourth seizure, but I decided not to tell the captain about my previous ones in college, and I had not had any during my basic training at Fort Wheeler.

I guess I was still in competition with my kid brother, Ed, because I said, yes, I wanted to stay in the Army.

My next stop after Fort Wheeler was Fort Meade in Maryland, where I took up the often lonely life of an infantry replacement. I was assigned to a barracks along with some fifty other replacements, none of whom I knew. In short order I learned something that would prove true throughout my stay in the Army: in any new group you could always find three or four guys you could relate to. But at Fort Meade, as at future locations, you never knew these guys for long. You would go to bed at night in a crowded barracks and wake up the next morning all but alone. Most of the others had "shipped out" during the night.

Shortly after Christmas of 1943, my next stop as a replacement was Camp Shanks, a few miles north of New York City, thence to His Majesty's transport *Ile de France*, then in British hands, along with a reported 12,000 other replacements. Instead of being part of a convoy, the *Ile*, too fast for a convoy, crossed the Atlantic alone, via a zigzag path (to avoid submarines, we were told) most of the way. My nights were spent at cards or in an upper bunk on the bottom deck with my nose less than a foot from a bulkhead.

Many of us survived on black market food sold to us by members of the English crew. To avoid such delicacies as rancid kidney stew and cold beef heart on the Army menu of the day, we stood in line for hours waiting to be herded into one of the crew's dining areas for lamb or beef sandwiches and hot tea, available for something like two dollars. I remember spending much of the rest of the day in hiding, usually without success, to avoid KP duty.

We landed in Scotland, on to Yeovil—Somersetshire, in the south of England—and the war. This is how I remember it 60 years later.

"Well," said one of the GIs sitting near me on the sunlit deck, "today I get a lot closer to combat than my old man ever got. He never got out of England."

"Hell," another GI said, "my dad never even got out of the United States."

"Neither did mine," said two or three of the others.

It made me think of my Uncle Al Larkin, who during World War I never even left Camp Dix, (as it was known then) a few miles from Trenton.

Normandy

It was D-Day plus 12.

Arriving in Normandy

There were about 250 of us aboard an LST (Landing Ship Tank) crossing the English Channel toward the French coast. We were all replacements—hapless, homeless, hopeless losers who had never been assigned to any unit—lost souls trained to take the places of GIs wounded or killed in combat. Twelve days earlier, on D-Day, June 6, 1944, Allied troops had landed on Normandy beaches against fierce, entrenched German opposition, and now—minus the hundreds who had already fallen—they were fighting their way inland.

At long last we were about to become members of some kind of established outfit, no longer lost souls. It was a good feeling: no more bivouacs, no more dry runs. From the way some of us were laughing and shouting on the deck of the LST, you might have thought we were on our way to a vacation on the Riviera. I admit I was one of the faux celebrants. The weather probably had something to do with it: a bright, sunny day, and a calm sea.

A few hours earlier our mood had been the same as we rode into Portsmouth, our port of embarkation on the southern edge of England. In our two-and-a-half ton trucks, in an endless line of other vehicles, we crept toward the port along a street crowded on both sides with people waving goodbye, mostly mothers with children. The women, many of them at second-floor windows, gave us V for Victory signs and wiped tears away.

"What the hell are they crying about?" a boisterous GI near me had kept shouting, and others had joined in. I remember one guy saying, "God, this is getting serious," and another saying, "That's the trouble with war; somebody's liable to get hurt."

One thing was for sure: it was a relief to know our monotonous and often lonely replacement days—into and out of one damned depot or training camp after another—was ended. No more chickenshit. ("At least there's not so much chickenshit in combat," more than a few had said during basic training.) No more passing through chow lines at unfamiliar camps and having "permanent KPs" joke about pissing on our graves. No more waking up to find myself in an almost empty barracks, with most of my fellow replacements (recently made friends, some of them) having moved out during the night. One of those departing had relieved me once of my Zippo lighter and a carton of cigarettes. At other stops along the way, wristwatches, pipes, and even crucifixes, one of them with Christ nailed to a cross made of blue-tinted strips of mirrored glass, disappeared in the night. Those days were over now; that was something to be thankful for.

An hour or more after boarding the LST, I was pleasantly surprised to find Sergeant Tom O'Hara aboard. O'Hara had been in charge of the I&R platoon at Camp Wheeler. We had developed great respect for O'Hara as he navigated us through basic training.

As our LST plowed on, O'Hara and I reminisced about those weeks: gathering intelligence about the enemy on patrols behind enemy lines, learning how to handle an M-1 rifle and bayonet—and especially about learning to hate the most mean-spirited son of a bitch in the United States Army, Ollie Goldsmith. Then he added some really bad news: "After you guys left, I was only at Wheeler for another seventeen weeks of basic. And one day there was a letter from Goldsmith. The son of a gun really was in Washington, DC! 'For the duration,' he said, and damned if he wasn't already a warrant officer!"

The news really spoiled my first day in France.

It was mid-afternoon of June 18, 1944, D-Day plus 12, when we reached the battered coast of Normandy, the stretch known as Utah Beach.

Troops landing Utah Beach, June 18, 1944

We climbed out of the transport into waist-high water and waded a hundred yards or more to the beach. There were many reminders of what had happened here twelve days earlier: everywhere the skeletons of demolished landing craft, minesweepers maneuvering through the clutter, and, on the beach, battered artillery pieces and deep shell holes. As we clambered up a worn path to high ground inland from the beach, a double line of German soldiers in green uniforms came into view. Some of them were laughing and waving at us. What the hell was this? They were bareheaded, no helmets. They were following another worn path that led down to the beach, an endless line of them, all with tanned faces, most of them chubby and looking healthier and better-fed than we did.

"How the hell are we gonna win a war against Bohunks like that?" somebody in our line said.

Farther on, we learned that they were mostly Poles who had been forced into the German army. Most of them had deserted at the first opportunity. They were to be taken to England as prisoners of war. But the war was over for them, the lucky bastards.

We were assigned to foxholes, and I was settling into mine when I heard an announcement over a public address system: "Private Dwyer! Private Dwyer!"

Our new homes

In a short time a corporal appeared at my side and said I was to report immediately to a lieutenant on duty "in that tent right over there." It was a large tent in a clearing of a wooded area.

"Private Dwyer?" the lieutenant asked as I entered the tent.

"Yes, sir."

He was seated a table loaded with papers, shaking his head over a file folder. "My God," he said, "I don't believe this."

I felt a shiver go down my back. Could this have something to do with the seizure?

Apparently he was amazed at the strange coincidence. "Whaddaya know! I interviewed you just last summer on your first day in the Army!" he said. "At Fort Dix!"

I remembered that day but I wondered what was coming.

"Here," he said. "Take a look; it's your service record."

And there is was; it had followed me all the way to England, and now to France.

The lieutenant told me that because of my experience as a newspaper reporter, as indicated in my file folder, I had been selected for a special assignment. I would be picked up first thing the next morning.

Hmmm. Guess I wouldn't be going on those reconnaissance patrols after all. Not exactly bad news. And maybe this time it would be *Stars & Stripes*.

The next morning, after an uncomfortable night in my foxhole—I discovered I had shared the hole with a foot-long lizard—I looked on as the other replacements were loaded into trucks that would carry them toward the front. Was I the only guy out of 250 not going? I experienced a vague feeling of guilt but dismissed it as nonsense. It wasn't as if I had asked for special treatment.

I tried to spot Sergeant O'Hara among the departing 250 but couldn't find him. Nor did I find Jimmy M., a youngster from Trenton. I had met him back in the staging area near Portsmouth a few weeks before we embarked for France. Along with many other replacements boarding the trucks, Jim would be killed in the fierce hedgerow fighting within a few weeks. After the war, I would spend an uneasy afternoon trying to explain the Army system to Jim's widowed mother back in Trenton: how some soldiers such as I were spared, and others, such as Jim, were not. She had several questions: Had Jim gone to Mass before leaving England? Confession? Had he received Holy Communion? I said yes and hoped it was true. Other questions were harder: What if Jim had gone to college? Wouldn't he have been less likely to be killed? Wasn't it true that college boys got safer jobs? I did my best to explain, but, from my experience I knew she certainly had a point. I watched as a mother tearfully blamed herself for not affording her son a college education.

After the last truck departed, I stood there alone, wondering about my special duty. Whatever it turned out to be, it would probably be less dangerous than the I&R job I had been trained for, first at Camp Wheeler, then Fort Meade (where I learned, among other things, to crawl under live machinegun fire), then further training at two camps in England.

Maybe it really would be a job with *Stars & Stripes* this time. No, probably not. I recalled a day a few months earlier, when I'd been called aside one morning for special duty. It was at the camp near Yeovil. Two of us had been summoned from the morning lineup and, instead of taking part in the day's training, we were ordered to report for special duty to a Captain X on the other side of camp.

Along the way, we considered the possibilities. The other guy said he had worked for a newspaper in Tucson. "No kidding?" I said. By the time we reached our destination, we were convinced, almost, that we'd soon be working for *Stars & Stripes*. Or maybe even *Yank,* the Army magazine.

It didn't turn out that way. The captain made that clear with his first question: "Either of you guys had any plumbing experience?"

Tucson and I spent the following two or three weeks far from the fields of our dreams—unclogging sewage drains. Morning after malodorous morning, we were given about a dozen flexible metal rods that we strung together to do the unclogging. Then we removed the first manhole cover of the day. Next one of us—we took turns—descended a long metal ladder and began poking at the clogged area. Some days it took a long time. Other days the drain burst free with the first or second poke. It then became a race up the ladder between the rod poker and the rising effluvium. I remember losing one of those races, and spoiling, among other things, the shine of my GI boots.

It was while retraining and plumbing at the camp near Yeovil that I heard some bits of war mythology. One was about the dumb private who went on sick call one day and was given a couple of suppositories for his constipation. He reported to the medic the next day that the suppositories had upset his stomach. "What!" said the medic raising his voice in exasperation, "You didn't swallow them, did you?"

"No, I stuck 'em up my ass!" was his sarcastic retort.

A true story, we were told, but didn't believe it.

Another was about an occurrence one night at a pub in Yeovil. It was noisy and crowded, but at one point the clamor subsided just as a GI was shouting, "Fuck King George!" In the silence that followed, an elderly Englishman made his way to the GI and, face to face with him, declared, "Fuck Babe Ruth!"

This one I heard from a GI who claimed he'd been in the pub when it happened. Swear to God.

Speaking of Yeovil, I remember it mostly as a popular place at night for outdoor sex. Many of the GIs believed that if you performed the act while standing, the girl would not get pregnant. Almost every storefront in the town was occupied at nightfall by such couples.

Right about here I should record an obscene but true World War II tale, certified by my friend Sam Cummings who was there when it happened. It was at a movie shown to an audience mostly of horny GIs in the South Pacific. At one point a curvaceous young woman in the film was killed. Immediately, from the audience, there came a loud admonition that brought on wild cheering: "Fuck her while she's still warm!"

* * *

A few minutes after the final truck departed for the front, I was picked up by a jeep.

"Private Dwyer?"

"Yes, sir."

"Hop aboard."

As I did, I noticed the driver wore two silver bars: a captain. He shook my hand and we were on our way. It turned out he wasn't sure what my assignment was. As we rode on, I was surprised at the number of dead cows along the way. Horses too, but not so many. Some wooden gliders that had brought GIs in on D-Day. No people at all in sight. Passing through a war-torn village (Ste. Mere-Eglise), where, I later learned, some 13,000 American paratroopers had dropped from the skies in the early hours of June 6, 1944 in support of the landings on Utah Beach. An American flag was unfurled at the town hall at 4:30 a.m., the first to be flown on French soil on D-Day. I noticed a huge crucifix standing tall and alone in a tangle of wires over what had been a church.

Within an hour or two I found myself seated at a typewriter and writing. But not for *Stars & Stripes*.

There were four of us, all privates, seated at typewriters in a room that reeked of cow dung in a ramshackle barn near the all but devastated village of Ste. Mere-Eglise in Normandy: Joe O'Keefe, a newspaperman from Wilmington, Delaware; Ira Brody, a businessman from Manhattan; a lawyer from Alabama (whose name I've forgotten), and me, a private who had been spared front-line duty because I had been a reporter for the *Trenton Times*. Our job was to write citations that would accompany Bronze Stars, Silver Stars, and other medals ranging up to Medals of Honor. The citations, based on reports from the front, described or attempted to describe acts of heroism: A sergeant "exposed himself to enemy fire in carrying a wounded soldier to safety"; a private "knocked out an enemy machinegun emplacement, enabling his unit to advance." The final sentence usually included something like "his valiant actions reflect great credit on himself and the Army of the United States." Writing these citations left you awed and feeling inferior to those up forward fighting the war. You'd think it often but never say it: "Christ, I'm glad I'm not up there."

As the days wore on, I came to know some things about the way the medal business sometimes worked. There were, for example, the Croix de Guerres the French Government had given the division for participants in D-Day. The French had suggested that 90 percent of the medals be awarded to enlisted men and 10 percent to officers. This, I was told, was promptly reversed, with officers getting 90 percent of them. I thought of a saying attributed to Napoleon: "Soldiers win the battles and generals get the medals." So what else was new? This was the Army, Mr. Jones.

I also came to know about captains and lieutenants who complained when deserving enlisted men in their units were overlooked for medals. The real reason, in too many cases, was that these lieutenants and captains were "too busy" to do the paperwork required.

One morning as the four of us were busy at our typewriters, we were joined by a fifth citation writer: a major, no less! Tall and black-haired, he reminded me of John Wayne. He appeared each morning in full uniform, head cast down, and took his place at one of the typewriters. He never said much and seemed preoccupied. His presence tended to make the four of us self-conscious. Our typewriters made the only sounds in the room.

Within a few days we learned some sad news: the major had panicked in combat, had run off in the face of the enemy—had, in Army lingo, "fucked up." He was on his way back to England, where he would be court-martialed.

A few silent days later he was gone.

What would happen to him? We all wondered. Prison? How would he explain to family and friends what he had done? How, I wondered, had he felt, writing citations about guys standing firm in the face of enemy fire and winning medals? I thought of him, especially as my eyes rested on his empty typewriter. I still think about him once in a while now, sixty years later.

In the days ahead, there was not much to write home about. There were the bottles, hundreds of them, of 4711 Cologne. They had become ours when the Germans abandoned them as they fell back. A strange aroma. We slept in tents set up on farmland and were sometimes endangered at night by roving cows. Never knowing or caring what day of the week it was. More dead cows and horses everywhere. Moving forward in trucks as the war advanced, being cheered by the Normandy farm families—and glared at by some (who didn't appreciate having their houses and barns demolished by artillery fire). The Normans had been treated well by the Germans, it was said. They'd behaved like gentlemen—most of them.

One day a two-and-a-half-ton truck arrived a short distance from where we were quartered. It was loaded with the corpses of GIs killed in the heavy hedgerow fighting. As we looked on in silence, the dead were carried to the edge of a nearby forest and laid in a row that stretched more than a hundred feet. They wore no helmets. Lying there, their faces tanned and healthy-looking as if asleep, they could have been taken for a line of sunbathers.

There were more trucks that day and the following days, bearing more of the dead. The bodies were carried off to be buried. I wondered how many of them had been among my group of 250 replacements who had come ashore a few weeks earlier at Utah Beach. And I thought about Warrant Officer Goldsmith back in his safe office in Washington, DC, the son of a bitch who said he would piss on the graves of such suckers.

Late one night a GI in a tent near mine shot himself in the foot with his M-1 rifle. "Oh, my god!" he screamed. "Help me! Help me!" He was still screaming and cursing as the medics carried him off. According to the next day's scuttlebutt, he'd shot his calf more than his foot, to avoid being returned to his company up front.

We made a happy discovery when division headquarters moved farther into Normandy to the area known as Calvados. The local farmers distilled a potent brandy from apples, and it was called—what else?—Calvados. Early one evening when five or six of us were sipping Calvados out in a wooded area, one guy reached a point beyond sipping. Something seemed to be troubling him; he became loud, almost boisterous. Then he spied a captain coming in our direction. "Gonna get that son of a bitch," he growled after taking a swig. He confronted the captain—the one who had picked me up from the beach a few weeks earlier—and took a wild swing or two before being stopped. The next morning he was sent to the front, and within a few days there was official word at division headquarters that he had been killed in action.

Saint-Lo

This is how Ernie Pyle, the famous war correspondent, put it: "If you don't have July 25 pasted in your hat I would advise you to do so immediately. At least paste it in your mind. For I have a hunch that July 25 of the year 1944 will be one of the great historic pinnacles of the war."

Pyle was referring to the beginning of the breakthrough at St.-Lo in which the Allied forces, led by our division, the Fourth, broke through the German lines and started advancing toward Paris and beyond. "It was the day we began a mighty surge out of our confined Normandy spaces, the day we stopped calling our area the beachhead, and knew we were fighting a war across the whole expanse of France."

Pyle "teamed up with the Fourth Infantry Division since it was the middle of the forward three divisions and spearheading the attack." He had been among the correspondents who were briefed on the July 25 operation. It was to open, he wrote, with "a gigantic two-hour air bombardment by 1,800 planes—the biggest, I'm sure, ever attempted by air in support of ground troops.

"It would start with dive bombers, then great four-motored heavies would come, then mediums, then dive bombers again, and then the ground troops would kick off, with air fighters continuing to work ahead of them."

It was about 10 o'clock in the morning of July 25, 1944, when the four-motored heavy bombers started passing overhead. The four of us citation writers left our typewriters and went to the apple orchard outside to witness an unbelievable show of force. The deep rumble of the planes reverberated in my chest. The line of heavies seemed endless.

Back at our typewriters, we resumed writing citations in silence. I could still feel the rumble.

After a few minutes Joe O'Keefe started chuckling to himself as he studied a sheet of paper in his hand.

"You guys are not going to believe this," he said, waving the paper over his head.

"Guess," he continued, "who's getting the Bronze Star!"—the medal created especially for combat infantrymen.

There were no ready guesses.

"The guy who digs the General's latrine!"

"No!"

"Under heavy enemy fire?"

"Why not a Silver Star?"

"What the hell, let's give him the Medal of Honor."

The banter continued until the door burst open, and there stood the adjutant general himself, and there was fire in his eyes. "Tenshun!" somebody yelled.

The four of us stood at our typewriters and froze at attention. In short order we were marched out to the apple orchard and ordered to stand at attention.

The AG, a short, barrel-chested lieutenant colonel, began pacing back and forth before us. "Those airmen up there," he said, pointing skyward, "they're doing their job. And so are the riflemen and artillerymen up ahead. And what are you doing down here? Telling jokes?

"Those men are fighting with real ammunition and real weapons. Back here, whether you know it or not, you are fighting a battle of another kind."

He paused, stopped pacing and looked us in the eye, one after another.

"Words!" he suddenly shouted. "Words, words, words, words are your ammunition." Pause. "Commas are your bayonets." Pause. "Sentences are your rifles." Pause. "Periods are your bullets."

He continued for what seemed a long time, and so did the heavies up above and the firing up ahead.

Then: "Right face!"

"March!"

In silence we marched from the apple orchard—left, right, left, right—back to our typewriters.

It turned out to be a long afternoon.

July, 1944

Dear Dwyers,

I was talking to another Frenchman today. He wanted to know what French news we had from the radio. I did my best to tell him what the allies were doing and it made him very happy. He was dressed like all the poor French I've seen—weather beaten cap, jacket and pants and wooden shoes. Some of them use straw inside the shoes in place of sox.

Americans at home would realize how lucky they are if they could see what war has brought to these people. Several days ago I passed through two towns. In one, not one building was intact and almost all buildings were leveled right down to the ground. In one particular area everything was completely ruined but in the center stood a crucifix about 30 feet high practically untouched. Along a road was a statue of the Blessed Mother still standing with a jar of faded flowers at its feet. There are similar statues at many road intersections all over France, they tell me.

In another town, Frenchmen, women, and kids were returning to what remained of their homes to salvage what was left of their belongings, and in some cases to look for possible remains of their missing. It would bring tears to your eyes to see a woman of about 90 taking a pair of blue trousers out of a battered bureau and brushing the dust off them. Or an old man poking through rubble with his cane looking for something; or another old man in tears after some Yanks gave him part of their rations. "The Germans take it away from us; you give us food," he says, shaking his head.

The Germans really did take it away. They simply helped themselves to everything—cows, pigs, horses, milk, butter, and sometimes they robbed so much wine that they used 15-and 20-year-old champagne to clean out mess kits. The French we have seen will never be able to forgive and forget.

An officer just came in with a bunch of flowers. A French kid had stopped him and presented the flowers: "Pour vous, Monsieur." It is typical of how the French feel about the Americans.

I'm getting anxious for news of all of you and of the whereabouts of brother Ed and brother-in-law Ed Schmierer.

Nan and Ed Schmierer, Dallas, Texas, June 1944, married six months

I take it Ed #1 is in India—or China. (When he was last home on leave he indicated one or the other would be his next assignment.) It will probably take months for us to exchange letters but I'll write him as soon as I get his address. Don't worry and keep writing.

All my love to all of you,
Bill

August 20, 1944

Dear Dwyers,

Your letters have been coming in regularly with Mother and Helen leading the pack. I got the pictures—Mother squinting, etc.—the other day. They were very good. I've been wondering how for one of the shots, you managed to get the Buick up on the front steps. It looks like a good trick. You'll have to show me.

There are a few items in the grocery line today which might interest you. One is that some of the local patriots have been handing out eggs and cognac for cigarettes which were tres scarce over here before the advent of the rich-bitch yanks. The underground has it that eggs, coffee—anything else except women and drink—are practically nonexistent in Paris. When the GIs take over Paris there will be plenty of cigarettes anyway. We're very well supplied with them.

"C'est la guerre" has apparently been replaced in the current unpleasantness, as the English say, by "C'est le Bosche". If a Frenchman is fresh out of something he would like to have sold or given to the Yanks, his explanation is usually "C'est le Bosche" with a nasty accent on the final word. Some are probably overworking the phrase as an explanation for any shortage, but I believe the exaggeration is slight if any. Contrary to what I've read in *Time* and other publications, the Germans weren't on their best behavior here. Comparatively so, perhaps, but from the word of what the infinitive splitters would call unimpeachable sources, I take it that the Germans were Germans and didn't qualify for any good conduct ribbons here.

Josef (of the egg & cognac Josefs) informs me that not long ago ten SS men, one with a revolver open for business, called at his home one morning and told him they were moving in. He has a small place and he showed me where the Nazis slept—he also pointed out the oversize closet which served as his own bedroom during the Germans' stay. Josef supports the statements of many others to the effect that the Germans took all the good wine they could gather before they took off. In general, it seems they took anything they might need and in as great a quantity that the speed of their retreat would allow.

Bernard, a 12-year old boy on "vacance" until school reopens "Premier Octobre," cites instances in which the Nazis forgot any etiquette they may have inadvertently picked up in Germany. A German officer walking through a small town would ask a prosperous-looking old man for the time. The Frenchman would either pull a watch out of his pocket or lift the sleeve over his wristwatch. The Nazi would thank him for the time, take the watch, and continue his stroll. Bernard says he saw it happen often. And, he says, it was the same with any item, small or large, which happened to catch a German's fancy.

Bernard got a kick out of telling us about some of the German aviators who had no planes in which to aviate. They "took off" he said, on horses and not planes when the Americans came. He then imitated a man on a horse trying to make a noise like an aeroplane. It was pretty funny.

Another Josef, this one a seminarian (Monsieur L'Abbe), says the reports of Nazi good behavior just ain't so. We met him when he was with an old French couple and a boy about seven. The boy, he said, had been more or less adopted by the couple almost two years ago. It seems the boy made the mistake of being born of Jewish parents. He has had no news of his parents since the Nazis took them off almost two years ago. Luckily he is too young to comprehend the situation fully. The Yanks gave him gum and candy and felt uncomfortable because that was about all they could do.

I am getting along much better with my French. The other night I had a French girl sitting on my left knee as I sipped some aperitif (which is the most delicious wine I've ever tasted). She told me I looked like some dentist she had known and liked. She called me dear in French and threw her arms around my neck. Not bad, eh? She was blonde and beautiful and her name was Yvette. I imagine she will be an interesting girl in 15 years when she will be 21.

I'm still at the same job, still like it very much. And latest information has it that I'm assigned. Take it easy. See you soon I hope.

All my love to all of you,
Bill

Paris

My most vivid memory of the next few weeks was Liberation Day in Paris. By the time our division reached the outskirts of the place, the lure of that city was overwhelming. My buddy Joe Costello of Chicago and I couldn't resist it. It was August 25, a month after the breakthrough at Saint-Lo, that Joe and I succumbed to the seduction of Paris, and thereby took the risk of ending our days as rear-echelon solders and perhaps ending our days on earth.

Division headquarters had moved within ten miles of the city, and the urge to see it proved irresistible. So we simply set out for a main highway, raised our thumbs, and in no time at all found ourselves in the midst of celebrating Parisians.

Unbelievable! There were cheers and kisses everywhere we went. French girls and their mothers lining up to kiss Americans and joyous crowds were singing the Marseillaise and yelling "Vive la France!" and "Vive L'Amerique!" A happy, sunny, summer day. We found it hard to believe we were really there. Paris! The City of Light. The Eiffel Tower! The Champs Elysees!

The sidewalk cafes were busy, but the only food available, it seemed, was onion soup. Parisians were complaining that, during the war, the Normandy farmers were more interested in providing food for German occupation troops than for French civilians. But such complaints were lost in the general celebration. At long last the Germans were gone.

But there was one scene that saddens me every time I think of it. A roaring mob is coming toward us. They're shaking their fists and shouting angry words we cannot understand. Then we see the target of the uproar: a sobbing woman. She is clutching an infant in one frail arm and attempting to protect her face with the other. All the hair has been shaved from her head. With lipstick a swastika has been drawn on her bald head. There are lipsticked swastikas on her cheeks as well. The mob passes on. The obvious is explained: she is the mistress of a Nazi officer.

There was life everywhere. Girls with skirts flying high, riding bicycles. The two of us walking along the Champs Elysees, gawking at the Eiffel Tower.

Back at division headquarters, after two unbelievable days, Joe and I waited for the reaction to our two days of Absent Without Official Leave (AWOL). What would the verdict be?

We didn't have to wait long. Our commanding officer, a captain named Book, called us into his office the day after our return. He told us that he had recommended to Colonel Castagnito, in command of division headquarters, that we be transferred as riflemen, to a company at the front. Both Joe and I remembered well the fate of the guy who punched a captain after downing too much Calvados.

For almost a week I found it difficult to sleep. Then we heard our fate: Colonel Castagnito decided that since it was the first offense for Joe and me, we could remain at our jobs in division headquarters. Whew!

Sept. 14, 1944
Somewhere in Europe

Dear Helen (sister),

I got my laundry back today from a lady in a nearby house. She did an excellent job. The stuff was filthy and she made it look like new. She pressed everything—shirts, pants, fatigues, handkerchiefs. And she wouldn't take any money for it. That's the way most of them are. We gave her rations, cigarettes and candy and she thanked us.

I believe I told you about the lady who owned the hotel. She wouldn't let us pay for the room either. Said it was an honor to have Americans stay there. Can't get used to this European hospitality.

I told you about Paris.

All my love,
Bill

Belgium

After Paris, we were headquartered in such Belgian towns as Saint-Hubert, Stavelot, and Spa, in that order. I was still writing citations for Silver Stars and other medals during the day and pulling guard duty every other night. There wasn't much to write home about.

One afternoon in Saint-Hubert another GI and I bowed and said, "Bonjour" to a couple of teenage girls. They smiled and responded, "Fuck you." (Some playful GIs had apparently given them lessons in English.)

In Stavelot we found a small hotel owned by a friendly Walloon family named Defays.

Stavelot

The place was off-limits, but five or six of us managed to find and sneak into it in the dark of night. There we spent hours drinking non-alcoholic beer, playing cards and sometimes singing. Occasionally I succeeded in staying overnight.

My romance with one of the Defays daughters, Agnes, had hardly begun when it was time for division headquarters to move on.

Agnes Defays

> Dear Family Dwyer
>
> I take the liberty on the occasion of the new year to present you my best wishes for 1946.
>
> I suppose that Bill has speak of his Belgian family. We are often thinking and talking about him and we regret that we have not know him before.
>
> He was a very good friend and my Mother and Father love him very much. I hope he is in good health and that it is the same thing for you.
>
> With kind regards I beg to remain, Sir, Madam Dwyer, yours most respectfully. Agnes Dehays

New Year's greeting to the Dwyers from Agnes

[Fall of 1944]

Dear Dwyers,

Just had another bath and rubdown—my 7th or 8th since coming here. The bath costs 15 Belgian francs (about 33 cents) and I would pay 100 if necessary.

During peacetime people come from France, England and the States for the mineral baths. No place exactly like it in the world, they tell us. It is supposed to be a treatment for anything from heart ailments to housemaid's knee. But the GIs aren't interested in its healing power. They bring along soap and make a real bath of it.

For 15 francs you get a private room about the size of our kitchen. You bathe in an oversize copper tub bubbling with natural gas at about 90 degrees or more. You get the feeling that you're stepping into a tub of boiling 7UP and it's quite a feeling.

An old guy with a long gray beard gives the rubdown (for 30 francs). Except one time when a masseuse did the job (three minute pause while Mother, Gran'mom and the 3 Twerps drop their jaws). The whole process really makes you feel good.

We're still sleeping inside and eating good food. There are no scales available but I've gained some weight since coming here. Chief reason is that we've found a place, safe from MPs, where we get steak, French fries, bread, butter and beer every night. It is a hotel managed by a very fine Belgian family who has practically adopted a couple of us for the duration of our stay here. At night they invite some of the local "Janes" in and we dance to "Anchors Aweigh" and "Yes, Sir, That's My Baby." The dancing wouldn't win any prizes but it's a lot of fun. One of the professors provides music on the piano. He's no lover of swing.

Not much else to report. It's raining, of course. Went to 10:30 High Mass yesterday.

Don't worry about me; I'm very safe. It's not a matter of whether but of how soon I'll be seeing you. And if things continue as at present I should be knocking at 572 in a few months.

All my love to all of you,
Bill

One afternoon, while walking along Spa's main street, I spotted a GI coming toward me who looked familiar. But who was it? A few steps farther on, I realized that it was me, as reflected in the front window of a store I was approaching. I hadn't seen myself full length, helmet and all, in such a long time that I had become a stranger to myself.

My only problem was that for almost a month there had been nothing at all for me at mail call. Nothing from Mother or Dad, nothing from my three sisters, or my brother Ed, nothing from Sandy Kerr, Ed McCardell, and other friends I'd been corresponding with. And then the news came.

Meanwhile letters had been flying back and forth from **Ed** to the folks back home.

August 1, 1944
(APO 467, Sta 7, NY NY)

Dear Folks,

I suppose you've probably noticed the new address. Yes sir, that's not a mistake; it seems that your #2 son is on the move again. But, I'll still be somewhere in India.

Mama, my sweet, I suppose you're guessing that I'll be going up to the "Hump." And you're guessing right. I'm moving to a base about 10 miles east of where Tom Nolan's stationed. I just missed his station but I do believe I'll be able to see him more now that we'll be so close. Please, don't start to worry about the Hump. I'll grant it's dangerous but no matter if you hit a 10 foot hill or one at 10,000 feet, you still don't bounce.

Now that I'm going up there I'm sorry I didn't get sent there in the first place because you're flying time counts double up on the Hump and your chances of getting home sooner are much better. I now have 1500 hours so maybe I'll be seeing you in about 10 months.

Dad mentioned about how Mother and all of you are going so regularly to church for Bill and me. Man, you don't know how proud that makes me feel and I certainly do appreciate it. Mama Dear, with the Lord and all of you pulling for Bill and me, I wouldn't worry too much about us. So Darling, it won't be too long before we'll both be home eating some of your marvelous food.

So, so long for now.

As always, all my love to all,
Ed

August 27, 1944
[censored]

Dear Folks,

I am now settled at my newest base here in India and I presume that I'll be here for a few months.

Haven't seen much of the Indian country here except to fly over it. About all we do is eat, sleep and fly, and once in a while take in a movie. I have flown the Hump quite a number of times and that's about all I can say, except that it's not bad at all.

Man, after seeing a bit of China (the Hump divides India and China), I can't say that it's much different from India. I'll guess it's more populated and just about as dirty.

The food is mainly C rations but I eat at least twice as much up here as I did at my last station. The weather is about the best thing we have and that is quite a relief from what we had before. I suppose that is the cause of my increased appetite. At night we need at least a sheet and sometimes a blanket feels mighty good. So you can see that it's quite a change from merely sleeping in the raw and sweating half the night.

I expected to see Tom Nolan on my way but I find that he's on his way home and will probably be home when you receive this. So some night you can pin him down and find out all about India. No doubt he'll have quite a collection of stories to tell but don't let them scare you. I'm a good 30 miles east of where he was, so I'll leave it up to him to explain where I am and what I'm doing.

The fellows here are as usual, the best, and everybody gets along as one big happy family. There are a lot of boys here I knew back in the States. So I can't say that I'm a stranger at all. And then again every time you fly you always run into someone you know.

I received quite a few birthday (Aug. 5) cards the past few weeks and I certainly appreciated them all. So thank everybody for me and I'll try to acknowledge them all later. Man it's hard to believe I'm 26.
    The censors don't allow me to say much about our work so you'll have to figure a lot of things out yourself. So don't worry when I don't write anything about flying.

This about does it for now and I'll be keeping you posted. I'm still in the pink and hope you are too.

So long for a while,

As always all my love,
Ed

The folks back home

Sept. 13, 1944 (from sister Helen)

Dearest Eddie,

Well dear, how're you doing by now? We had a very nice letter from you today and we were more than glad to hear that you're still okay. We had a letter from Willie too, so it was a big day in the Dwyer household. He's in Germany; at least, that's what we gather. From all reports the 4th Division was the first division to land in Germany. So after this is all over you and Willie will be able to hold your own whenever the subject comes up "and where were you in the last war?" Bill said he received a letter from you and you from him so it's nice to know that you're finally catching up with each other. Boy won't it be nice when you two finally meet and try to out-talk each other. That will really be the day.

Sunday's paper announced the engagement of Tom Nolan to Virginia Christie. Everyone was expecting it sooner or later so it didn't come as much of a surprise. She had a ruby with a diamond on either side—different—don't you think? They plan to be married in a few weeks if Tom stays in Tennessee where he is now. Does India make a boy want to get married?

There was an article in *Life* magazine all about the Hump and one in *Reader's Digest*. It sure gets a lot of publicity and describes its pilots as keen, steady and smooth but it really gave us the creeps when we read about it so please be careful. We're saving all of the articles so you can compare notes when you return.

Well dear, it's time for dinner. I only wish you could be here to join us but you will someday soon. Be good and write soon,

Love,
Helen

PS. Peg Murphy was in the store today and wanted to be remembered to you.

On September 28, 1944,
Mom sat down and wrote this letter.

My dear Eddie,

Received your letter of the 27th a couple of days ago, but as the girls were writing, I thought I would write a different date. I am so glad dear you are getting your mail, and that you generally receive two or three letters when you come back from your trips. I do wish you could receive your boxes. We sent some when you first went over, then we sent more for your birthday. It didn't seem to take so long for your gifts to come through. My, everyone really raves about them. We say they are hand inlaid and hand carved and think they are made of ivory. Can you tell us anything more about them? They certainly are beautiful.

Eddie in one of your Xmas boxes I put in a bottle of 100 vitamin capsules. I went up to Petty's and the druggist told me what kind to get. Now they are quite expensive, but he says they are really good. He said to tell you to take two a day and they should supply any deficiency in your diet. Mrs. Bruther said when their Johnnie came home he was a nervous and physical wreck. So the doctor put him right on these pills and egg and milk. I know it is impossible for you to get eggs and milk, but I do wish Eddie, if you ever get them that you will take them faithfully. If there is anything else that you know that we can send you please request it.

Well dear, the news hasn't been so good lately. Even Gabriel Heater doesn't think it will be over this year. I am enclosing a clipping telling where Bill's 4th Division is. I am afraid they are in a pretty bad spot. However, I think Bill, being in Headquarters, is a little safe.

It seems like a strange thing to say, but I am glad you are kept busy, but outside of getting your hours in faster, I know the best thing for all of us is to keep too busy to think. Imagine dear you having 1,500 hours in the air. I know you are a good flyer and am counting on that to bring you home safe and sound. Along with our prayers, and I know you say a few yourself.

Grandmom had a little spell of gall bladder trouble last Saturday and Sunday. We had Dr. Murphy a couple of times, but now she feels pretty good again. The pain is all gone, but she is a little weak yet. She certainly has wonderful health for her years, and sure comes back quick.

All the Larkin boys (cousins) are all right so far. I guess the only one in real danger is Eddie, and they are quite sure he is in Gen. Patton's tank crew. Not so good.

Write whenever you can dear, it is grand to know you are all right.

God love you dear,
Mother

It wasn't until much, much later that I finally got all the details of exactly what happened at 572 Bellevue Avenue on October 7, 1944.

There was a light breeze punctuating the sunny autumn afternoon. Mom was upstairs looking out the window at the sugar maple bursting with vibrant color. She noticed a car slowly turning into the drive.

When the bell rang, Helen who was home early, yelled "I'll get it!"

The uniformed officer was visibly uncomfortable. Young, crisply dressed but at the core just another soldier doing his job. "I'm so sorry," he said and gently handed her the telegram. Helen stood there at the open door while the bottom dropped out of her world. She couldn't speak and finally after a minute or so the officer simply turned and walked back to the waiting car.

She slowly closed the massive wooden door until it clicked and then gingerly peeled back the sealed envelope with its hideous message. "We regret to inform you . . ."

It was then that the keening started, beginning as a small mewling that rose to a full-bodied wail of primordial pain.

She turned and slumped against the closed door. Only then did she see her mother waiting quietly on the bottom stair, her hand clutching the newel-post, her face a study of frozen acceptance, an expression that would visit her often over the years to come.

"Which one?" she whispered.

"Eddie." Helen cried. "His plane crashed."

And before any of a hundred questions could be asked, questions that would never have any suitable answers, my mother fainted.

Several days later the letters from Helen and Mom were returned unopened along with Eddie's last letter home, oddly enough dated September 28, two days before he died.

> Dear Folks,
>
> Just a short note to let you know that things are still about the same in the charming country called India. I suppose I can at least pray that this will hit the States somewhere around the 10th of October. I do believe on that day Pop will be at least 35. So congratulations Pop and come your next birthday we'll be able to have a few quickies. Enclosed find a check for $100 on a money order. You know what to do with it. I would like to send you something but it's next to impossible to get anything up here. I did send you something for Christmas so someday you should find something in the mail.
>
> It's finally stopped raining and today was a beautiful day. As usual we're doing quite a lot of flying and this still pleases me greatly because the more flying we do the sooner we get home. And it gives you a thrill to think that you're really doing something to get this mess finished. As far as being dangerous I can't see it and don't believe it's any more dangerous than the flying I did before. So forget about worrying about me and just pray that this time next year we'll all be home swapping stories.
>
> You know I've finally figured something you can send me. I and my tent mates would really appreciate any food delicacies, such as canned chicken, crab meat, sardines, pickles, pickled pig's feet or anything

similar. It seems that our diet is not the best to be had and any kind of a diversion would be great.

Love and kisses,
Ed

First Lieutenant Edward Thomas Dwyer, Jr.

[Below is an upbeat letter home from Bill also trying to allay their fears, unaware that the same day his family was learning of Ed's death.]

October 7, 1944
Letter from Bill

Dear Folks,

Mother seems to be worrying a bit—and without good reason. Remember, I'm strictly a headquarters man and am in the rear. I'm in no more danger than you. Further I'm living inside sleeping on a mattress and working in a steam-heated room. Until now I was still sleeping in the forest—rain or shine. I had slept in a bed twice since coming to Europe, once in Paris and again in a small hotel where the Germans had often slept and, from the looks of things, had often had indoor target practice. There were bullet holes in the walls and ceiling. The woman who operated the place said they did the same in other hotels in the city. We expected to pay for the room but the lady wouldn't take our money. She said it was an honor to have Americans in her place.

The mattress, pillow and clean sheets almost made me think I was home again. Further No. 2: we're on B rations again. And tomorrow we get our first oranges. Imagine, a real orange.

So I hope you see there is no point in worrying.
We got an extra blanket and winter underwear today. Soon we get our overcoats.

We were paid today and with what I drew, & had returned from borrowers, I now have $45 but not dollars. It's just like the "invasion" money we used in France in that it was printed in the States. Enclosed is one mark which is worth 10 cents. A pound is $4, a French franc is worth 2 cents and a Belgian franc is 4 cents. You learn something new every day. Now all I need is something to spend it on. I'd like to get something good for all of you but so far I haven't had the opportunity. I'm afraid my box will look like a 5&10 shoplifter's haul compared to Ed's.

When you read about Paris, remember that only a small percentage of troops are there for any time. The 4th was lucky even to pass through and even 4th men got there only once or twice. They were glad to see us & the GIs were pleased to have somebody make a fuss over them because it has been a long time between fusses. I would still like to get back there someday and look up the people who practically adopted Costello (buddy) and me during our stay.

Helen and Del seem to be taking my comments about the gals in Paris too seriously. In fact, it seems that all the American gals are up in arms about it. There was a big article in the *Stars & Stripes* about it. One U.S. girl said, "If they kiss an old guy like Ernie Pyle, what must they do to the young soldiers?" We couldn't help it in Paris but I guess I'll take American gals.

To prevent any shortage in the far future I'll again request cigarettes & candy. We got two packs today but I'll be back on butts again by Wednesday. Take it easy & don't take Gabriel Heater too seriously, nor Drew Pearson. Thanks for your wonderful letters.

All my love to all of you,
Bill

It was a late October morning when I received the letter from Mom, and it began with a sentence that almost obliterated me on the spot: "Our poor dear Eddie has been killed." Her tears had dropped and blurred the blue ink of the words that followed. But there was no mistaking it. He had died Oct. 1, 1944.

Eddie was twenty-six, two years younger than me. He had been "flying the Hump" over the Himalayas—delivering supplies from India to Chiang Kai-shek's troops in China for some time. The last time I had seen him was almost a year earlier on what turned out to be his next to last visit home. Among other things he told me was that on his latest flight to China, he had been carrying broomsticks and Ping-Pong paddles and balls to be used by the Chinese troops.

My kid brother, the warm, openhearted, reliable, happy-go-lucky guy who was always a winner at cards and with girls as well, was dead. No! There must be a mistake. Not Eddie! Any day now there would be a letter explaining it was all a mistake. Such things happen in wartime, I told myself. With all the dying and confusion of war, there were reports that turned out to be false. But, as I continued to read Mom's letter, the lump in my throat seemed to expand.

As I read the letter over and over, tears in my eyes, the lump almost choking me, I could see Eddie clearly: playing golf with Dad and me; riding Red, his favorite horse; and, just a few months ago telling the family about his Army Air Corps job: piloting a transport plane over the Hump from India to China and back. The irony was that he had re-enlisted a year before.

Now he was gone, his plane having developed serious trouble and crashing in China, as I later would learn. The lump in my throat would remain for many days turning into months, as I really cried night after night. I don't remember how I got through the first week and those that followed. He was my only brother and my best friend.

The two of us

Eventually the details of Ed's death unfolded via a letter from Bub Travers, serving in China, to his father, friends of our family in Trenton.

Late October 1944

Dear Dad,

I had not heard about Ed Dwyer being killed but was able to find out about his accident very quickly.

He had quite recently been checked out as first pilot on C-46 (Commando) airplanes and he was killed while on a trip. He was en route from his home station, Sookerating, to one of the secret B-29 bases with a load of gasoline—100 octane. On these trips, to deliver the greatest load, it is necessary to stop after crossing the Hump to pick up additional gasoline. On this particular night, Ed arrived at one of the bases in China (Luilang] to refuel before going on to Changtu. He then taxied out for takeoff. Just after leaving the ground, one of his engines failed. This is the most critical time in flying—from the time the wheels leave the ground until the airplane attains sufficient speed to enable it to continue flying in the event of an engine failure. It usually lasts anywhere from 30 to 45 seconds. However Ed lost an engine before he could attain sufficient speed to continue flight on one engine. Apparently he was quite cool and collected because he picked up his microphone and called the control tower and told them exactly what had happened. He then told the radio operator to go to the tail of the plane and brace himself for a crash landing (the tail is the safest place to be in case of a crash). From then on it was just a question of how soon they would hit. When the airplane did crash it immediately caught fire. The radio operator was thrown clear and is still alive. Both Ed and his copilot were killed instantly in the crash. The accident occurred very shortly after midnight.

There is nothing else to tell you about the accident. It was just one of those things that are going to happen until they make engines that don't stop running.

Well, Dad, I hope that this will be sufficient to explain just how Ed was killed. Please give his family my deepest sympathy and tell them that the job Ed was doing is what makes possible the raids by B-29's on Japan.

Lots of love,
Bub

One of the few other things I remember of that day is going to a church nearby and arranging for a Mass to be said for Eddie early the next morning.

I was a true believer in those days, or was I? The seeds of doubt sown at Trenton State had begun to sprout, but as they say, there are no atheists in foxholes. And it was so important to my family that I be a good Catholic, so I dutifully went through the motions.

It was a 7 a.m. service; I recall the priest would take no payment for it and that I was not present. Around midnight we were ordered to prepare to move, and a few hours later we were on our way to the next stop on our way to Germany.

Luxembourg

To Luxembourg City, as it turned out, the capital of the grand Duchy of Luxembourg. Within a few days, there was some good news: I was to become the *Stars & Stripes* reporter for the division.

Reporting the War Scene

Back in July of 1944, I sent off a column about the Fourth Division to the *State Gazette,* a paper I had worked for before the war. It was titled "From Fort Dix to France," and it recounted some of the exploits of the division in landing on D-Day and taking part in the breakthrough at Saint-Lo. The column was picked up by the division's clipping service, and in early autumn it resulted in my being given the job of covering the division for *Stars & Stripes.* No more citations to write, and I'd meet some interesting people.

As a correspondent for *Stars & Stripes* with the Fourth Division, I was well aware, as were many other GIs, that Ernest Hemingway, the famous author of *The Sun Also Rises,* was among us. But I did not know until after the war that two other famous writers had been members of the Fourth. One of them was John Cheever, who would be author of such novels as *Oh What a Paradise It Seems* and *The Wapshot Chronicle.* Cheever had been with the Fourth when it was training in the South but was transferred to another unit when the division went overseas.

I was acquainted with another man who was to become an acclaimed author, but during the war I had no idea that he was even interested in writing. His name was Jerry Salinger—yes, the famous but elusive J.D. Salinger, author of *Catcher in the Rye* and best-selling collections of short stories.

Salinger was with the Fourth Division's 12th Regiment when it landed on Utah Beach on D-Day. He was a Counter Intelligence Corps (CIC) lieutenant and with other CIC men was assigned to division headquarters. During the Fourth's advance, village after village was captured. As each place was overrun, the CIC men carried out their special duties: taking over the government of the captured towns, searching for collaborators, grilling prisoners of war.

The Fourth Division captured thousands of German soldiers as it advanced through France, Belgium, Luxembourg, and into Germany. One day in the early spring of 1945, I was told the 50,000th prisoner taken by the Fourth was being held at division headquarters. A good story, maybe.

Number 50,000 turned out to be a tall, skinny blond German enlisted man who, to my surprise, spoke with confidence and even enthusiasm. Standing bareheaded and almost at attention, he readily answered the questions put to him by Salinger and another CIC man. In the prisoner's view, the war was far from over. In fact, he said, the real war was just beginning. For now the Americans and British would join with the Germans and fight the Russian Communists.

This was the last-gasp line that the defeated Hitler was putting out, according to the CIC, and almost every prisoner taken recently said the same thing. It was time to defeat the real enemy, Russia. Number 50,000 appeared to be sure that would really happen.

The story I wrote about the interview eventually appeared in *Stars & Stripes* after it had been pared down to two or three paragraphs. Even so, I was thankful it appeared at all, space being so tight in the Army daily.

It wasn't until after the war, in 1951, that I learned that CIC lieutenant Jerry Salinger was a writer. I also learned he'd sold stories to *Esquire* and other magazines before and during the war, and that one of his most memorable short stories, *For Esme—with Love and Squalor,* was based on an incident when the Fourth Division was preparing for D-Day at Tiverton, in Devon, England.

With Captain William Bouton, the division's PRO (Public Relations Officer), and a couple of others, I was riding toward the front in a jeep one afternoon early in December 1944. As we advanced, a V-2 rocket, emitting its raspy roar, streaked like a lightning bolt across the sky. A few seconds later we could hear the explosion as, miles behind us, it crashed to the ground. The V-2 was the Nazis' latest "miracle weapon," a successor to the V-1, the "vengeance weapon."

We had been hearing a lot about "buzz bombs"—jet-propelled rockets that were pilotless and remotely controlled. Launched from a site in northern Germany, they carried a ton or more of explosives at a speed of more than 300 miles an hour. The first V-1 had hit London back in June 1944.

The even deadlier V-2 started bombing in September. Now it was being aimed at targets in Belgium and Luxembourg.

As we rode on, a second V-2 roared across the sky, prompting a surprising reaction in the area we were approaching: dozens of GIs were celebrating—reaching for the sky and appearing to be cheering the V-2 on! What the hell was this?

On closer inspection we learned the answer. It was in what the GIs were shouting: "Hurray! Maybe that one'll get some of the rear echelon bastards." "Hurray! It's their turn now!" "It's about time."

I was shocked at first; after all, I was one of the rear-echelon bastards. Later, thinking it over, I concluded that if I had been in their shoes, in their foxholes, day after perilous day, I'd probably have been cheering, too.

I was not a prestigious staff reporter like Jimmy Cannon or Andy Rooney, just a lowly division reporter hoping to get some accounts about the Fourth's accomplishments into the limited columns of the Army daily. I made four or five carbon copies of each article I wrote: one for *Stars & Stripes*, one for Army radio, one for hometown newspapers, and so forth. Breaking into the limited columns of *Stars & Stripes* was an almost impossible task. (There were complaints from many front-line soldiers about lack of coverage, including a letter to the editor written by a GI who lamented that the only time his outfit had been mentioned in the paper was when a fellow member was hanged for rape.)

Speaking of Jimmy Cannon, one of his articles in *Stars & Stripes* caused some arched eyebrows among readers and threatened a rupture in relations between the United States and the Grand Duchy of Luxembourg. Cannon's opening sentence, to the best of my recollection, noted that Luxembourg City was graced by "seven beautiful bridges." This was followed by other impressive statistics. Then: "and the oldest whores in the world." Cannon went on to report that several taverns in downtown Luxembourg City employed as bartenders two or three females of a certain age who were available for further duty upstairs. (Indeed, in a popular tavern in Luxembourg City, one afternoon after the war in

Europe ended, I found two sixtyish females not only on duty at the bar but also available for second-floor gymnastics.)

As a *Stars & Stripes* reporter, I was now part of the Public Relations Office, a miniscule unit of division headquarters and headed by Captain Bouton. Shortly after that V-2 experience, he was reassigned as a company commander with the division's Eighth Regiment at the front. He was succeeded as PRO by Lieutenant Arthur Milton, formerly an executive with the *New York Daily Mirror*, and like Bouton, a respected officer.

The Hemingways

Earlier in the war, PRO had been home base for Ernie Pyle and other well known correspondents. Now, for some time, it had been the home office for the celebrated author Ernest Hemingway, who was covering the war for *Collier's* magazine, usually accompanied by a *Collier's* photographer named Joe Dearing. Hemingway had been with the Fourth—off and on but mostly on—since the time of the Normandy invasion. He had travelled with the doughs of the Fourth as they helped to spearhead the St. Lo breakthrough, when they took part in the liberation of Paris, and when they helped to break the von Rundstedt offensive, an effort by the Germans led by Field Marshall Gerd von Rundstedt to secure France. He was just back from two weeks of the bloody Hurtgen Forest battle where he'd been the guest of his idol, Colonel Charles "Buck" Lanham, commanding officer of the Fourth Division's 22nd Regiment.

In December 1944, with Hemingway as our star boarder, we were occupying a large house in a suburb of Luxembourg City. One day I was having a C-rations lunch in the kitchen with Joe Dearing, Hemingway's photographer. Dearing, who liked my stuff, had just finished reading a carbon copy of a story I'd sent off to *Stars & Stripes*. "Good piece," he said.

Just then, Hemingway came into the kitchen, emitting an enormous yawn. He had been in bed all morning, a frequent practice of his; sometimes he remained in bed all day.

"Here," Dearing said, handing him the copy. It was only about a page. I held my breath as Hemingway looked it over while stroking his beard. It seemed to take a long time.

Finally, he turned to me and said, "Not bad."

I exhaled happily. "Not bad" from Hemingway was not bad at all.

Ernest Hemingway

I remember "Papa" Hemingway during one of the happiest periods of his life. He was a certified celebrity, a combat veteran who had liberated Paris, and a celebrated author then working as a correspondent. He was like a child in a candy store. I remember several times when I, a lowly *Stars & Stripes* reporter, rode toward the front with him, feeling lucky to be in such company. Each time our jeep appeared, with the top down so all could have an unobstructed view of the great man, GIs—sometimes dozens of them—would give him a hearty welcome.

Papa was hard to miss near the front. For one thing, he usually didn't wear a helmet, and that huge head of his and purple-red face stood out like a beacon. Just the sight of him smiling confidently and casually moving forward seemed to reassure the GIs. They were not alone, not as long as Papa was there, riding in the front passenger seat of his jeep, and waving to them. Papa! In person! Yes, his jeep. The top brass of the Fourth Infantry Division—his division—was happy to provide a jeep or two for him as well as a cook and a driver—and plenty of gin for his canteen (sometimes gin for one canteen and dry vermouth for the other)—whatever

Papa wanted. Papa never lacked for anything when he was with the Fourth, which was most of the time he spent in the European theater of operations during World War II.

One afternoon I was riding with him and a few others near the front when, out of nowhere, a fighter plane headed in our direction. "Oh, my God!" somebody yelled, and we all ducked—all except Hemingway. The plane proved to be one of ours, and the pilot, we figured, was merely buzzing us. No problem. Hemingway, I noted, took it all in stride and didn't even comment on it then or afterwards.

Late one morning riding forward in our jeep, we encountered some riflemen up ahead. One of them, recognizing Hemingway, yelled "Hey, it's Papa!" Quickly the word spread and they were all yelling "Papa!" and cheering. Hemingway enjoyed talking to them about "the damn Krauts." As we departed, one of them yelled, "Come back soon, Papa," and others joined in until we were out of sight.

There were a few nights when we just sat at Hemingway's big feet and listened to his comments and stories, or occasionally to his answers to questions about writing. Samples: "Don't stop writing until you've reached a point where you can easily resume writing the next day." "Write what you know; no bullshit; just tell it straight and true."

I didn't like some of his stories, such as one he told about an incident shortly after D-Day back in Normandy. One afternoon, he said, he had come upon a young lieutenant who was so rattled by heavy enemy fire that he couldn't make up his mind whether or not to move his men forward. "I just gave him a good kick in the ass," Hemingway said, laughing, "and he got moving." I remember wondering whether the lieutenant and his men had survived the move.

Hemingway was obviously proud of his ability to stay cool and think clearly under pressure while others were losing their nerve. But he apparently failed to realize the difference between the plight of that lieutenant responsible for the men under his command and that of a correspondent with no such responsibilities. On that afternoon in Normandy, it was a simple matter for Hemingway: just kick the lieutenant in the ass and move on.

At times Hemingway seemed unaware of another difference: that unlike a front-line soldier, he could always go back to the relative safety of the rear—in company with us rear-echelon bastards. My observation was that he had absolutely no sense of humor and took himself very seriously. (Years later, his fourth and final wife, Mary Welsh, reminded him, during heated arguments, that he had never really been a soldier. "You've never been anything but a combat voyeur—a war watcher," and, "You've never been in the uniform of any army or air force.") A.E. Hotchner, a close friend, noted these charges in a postscript to his biography *Papa Hemingway*.

One day late in 1945 Hemingway informed a group of us that his kid brother was about to become a member of our division—in fact, a member of our PRO unit. In addition to other tasks, Hemingway had no doubt managed the coming transfer. "My brother's unhappy back there in Paris," he said. "He's in a film outfit with Saroyan and Shaw and some other goddam four-effs, and he wants to get up here and see some of the real war before it's too late." The four-effs he was referring to were authors William Saroyan and Irwin Shaw, apparently not among his favorites. (Years later I would learn that Shaw had been a lover of Mary Welsh and had introduced Hemingway to her.)

Bill with Papa's little brother,
Leicester Hemingway, after the war

A few days later Leicester (Les) Hemingway arrived—a clone of his older brother (older by about 17 years): same rugged build, same moustache, same broad smile. For a moment or two I wondered whether I should salute before shaking hands with him. I was just a private first class, and Leicester had to be an officer of some kind. He was wearing what appeared to be an officer's field jacket, possibly Canadian, sharply pressed trousers, and British leggings over glistening boots.

Actually, as a PFC I outranked him; Les, it turned out, was a mere private.

The next morning, elder brother asked me to show younger brother around the division a bit, and I proceeded to get a jeep and do just that. I noticed that Les was no longer wearing the officer's jacket. (Nor did I ever see him in it again.) About noon we found ourselves in company with members of a tank-destroyer outfit—grizzled combat veterans who reminded me of the bearded Willies and Joes depicted by Bill Mauldin in *Stars & Stripes*. A chow line formed shortly after we arrived, and Les and I were invited to join it.

As we waited in the line, metal mess gear in hand, I noticed Les had raised his voice a decibel or two. Some of the GIs in line turned tentatively in his direction. Who the hell was this guy?

Then, without preamble, Les blurted out something that got their stunned attention. "No wonder my father blew his brains out," he said. "I'll bet my mother was the worst lay in the whole damn country." Now the Willies and Joes were asking, or answering, the same question: "Hear what that guy said about his mother and father?"

Les quickly became known for talking to be overheard, often about private matters. Calling attention to himself, he wanted everybody to know he was a Hemingway.

It is true Dr. Clarence E. Hemingway, father of Ernest and Leicester, committed suicide with a revolver shot to the head in 1928 when Les was thirteen years old. That afternoon Les had been in bed recovering from a cold "when he hard the loud WHAMP that seemed to come from the other end of the house." In his autobiographical novel, *The Sound of the*

Trumpet, he continued: "He jumped out of bed and opened the door. At the end of the hall the door to his parents' room was closed. He ran down the hallway and someone called up, 'What was that?'

"'It sounded like a shot.'

"He knocked on the door. 'Daddy!' He tried the door. It opened, and in the darkened room, all shades drawn except one, there on the bed lay his father, making hoarse breathing noises. His eyes were closed, and in that first instant as he saw him there in the half-dark, nothing looked wrong. He put his hand under his father's head. His hand slipped under easily and when he brought it out again, it was wet-warm with blood.

"'Oh, Daddy, Daddy.'"

One morning shortly after Les joined our PRO group, he invited me to take a ride with him. Minutes later we were sailing along in a jeep he'd been assigned for the day. He was being tried out as Division photographer, to replace Jim Kimbrough, who had recently graduated from the job. His destination was the headquarters of the burgomaster of a German town. We reached the town in a short time and soon found the burgomaster's headquarters. As we got out of the jeep, I noticed that Les was carrying a barracks bag.

"What the hell's that for?" I asked.

"You'll see."

The burgomaster was in his office, and Les, in his fractured German, proceeded to explain his mission: to inspect the arms that the townspeople had turned in. Where were they?

The burgomaster, rubbing his hands nervously, led us to a large room that was all but bursting with armament—rifles, shotguns, pistols, revolvers, swords. All in a pile that almost reached the ceiling.

A first-class opportunist, Les immediately started filling the barracks bag with the arms. He would repeat this procedure whenever a jeep was available and another town had been overrun.

The Krauts developed a jet fighter plane several months before we did, and one afternoon Leicester Hemingway and I got a glimpse of one. We were inside a house in Luxembourg when we heard its roar nearby. We raced to the nearest window in time to see it buzz the house. Wow, what speed! As we ran toward another window for a further look, Les bumped into a table and fell to the floor, injuring his knee.

The next day he applied for a Purple Heart.

For a glimpse of Les in the early days of his time at Division headquarters, let's return to *The Sound of the Trumpet* and his alter ego, Dan Granham, "a private writing feature stories for an army newspaper." He goes on to report that "by going along on night patrols, he got to see a good deal.... And when he came back to Division headquarters, he found that his stories provoked a good deal of interest, and he had access to more information than he had ever had before. When the paper used things he had written, the men in the line companies were impressed, and single issues that moved forward were given maximum hand-to-hand appreciation."

It wasn't long before it became obvious that he had more interest as a collector, presumably running the guns on the black market, than as a combat soldier. What to do with Les? Lieutenant Milton decided, after trying him at other work, to make him our photographer and occasional jeep driver.

Les set off on foot most days, supposedly in search of photo opportunities, often without film in the camera—sometimes riding when a jeep was available. He went out almost every day as division photographer and collector of guns and worked on his book nights. Les had his wife send him special cameras. Occasionally he'd come back with war stories nobody believed.

One day late in February, Papa and his jeep driver, Archie Pelky, dropped by on their way back from Paris. Papa had been cleared there of a charge that he had used firearms, a no-no for correspondents.

This time he left behind a couple of young Frenchmen. Temporarily they were added to our group. One was Jean DeCamp, about thirty, who had worked as a cameraman for

Pathe' News before the war. The other was Richard, in his early twenties. Both were members of the anti-Nazi French Forces of the Interior (FFI). They had been members of Ernest Hemingway's much publicized "irregulars" back in the days leading up to the Allies' taking of Paris—a group of French partisans who were established as an informal command force, a kind of fan club, for scouting enemy territory and addressing the big man as "Mon Capitaine."

Jean and Richard busied themselves with scrounging a living during the day. Les and I were with them at night, playing cards, or just swapping stories in our fractured French. They were interesting, likable guys, and the four of us became friends.

Late one afternoon Les and I came back from a day of exploring story possibilities. We returned to our room and found it stripped of almost everything we owned: all our blankets, sheets, and clothing were gone! What the hell had happened? Our French buddies undoubtedly made a small fortune on their return to Paris. Such items as blankets were going for the equivalent of hundreds of dollars in the booming black market there.

Papa was through with the war. He was through with his job as a *Collier's* correspondent covering the war, through with carrying that .45 caliber pistol, through with playing war, through with acting the role of Papa for the soldiers of the Fourth Division.

He was never an actual participant in combat . . . under orders of an officer. In WWI he was an ambulance driver. In the Spanish Civil War he was not a member of the Lincoln Brigade but a correspondent. In WWII he was not an officer responsible for his actions but a correspondent with his own little army, a bunch of "freedom fighters" who were thieves. It eventually dawned on me. *He's no more hero than I am.* He's just as naïve about combat as I am . . . figuring others'll get hit but not me.

It took several trips to the supply sergeant to replace what our friends had taken. We wondered what they could get for our stuff on the very active black market in Paris.

Rothenburg

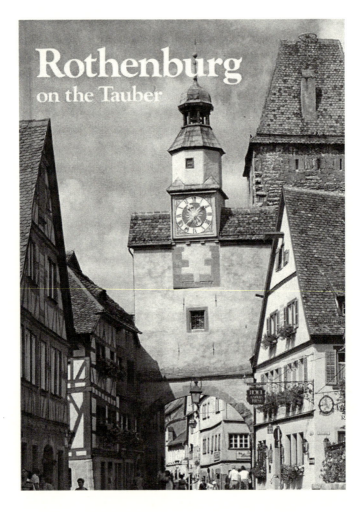

It was about quarter past three in the afternoon—"15:15 hours" in the Army lingo that I never got used to—when I arrived at the command post of the First Battalion, Twelfth Regiment, Fourth Infantry Division. The battalion commander himself, Major Frank Burk, greeted me, and I could tell from previous visits he was, as usual, in a frisky mood.

"Well," he said, "this time we really have a story for you. We're sending a truce party into Rothenburg, and you're just in time: we need one more volunteer."

I thought he was kidding. The last time we'd met, a couple of weeks earlier, I reported encountering sniper fire on the way up. "It's about time you rear-echelon guys saw some action," Burk had said, but with a wink and a smile.

With a flush of excitement, I realized that this time he was serious: I was to become a member of a white-flag patrol into Rothenburg. Wow! But along with the excitement, I experienced a vague sign of possible trouble ahead—that dizzy feeling that I had come to think of as a "swirl." In the past it had indicated a possible seizure, but it passed.

And now, on a sunny April afternoon in 1945, I was about to join a patrol into Rothenburg, Germany, a medieval walled city about 200 feet above the valley of the Tauber, as I would later learn, with a population of about 13,000.

I was ecstatic, and not at all concerned about the possibility of a swirl. At long last I, a rear-echelon bastard, was about to get in on some action. I hurried out of battalion headquarters to report the change of plans to Sergeant John Hufford, who was waiting in our PRO jeep. A wounded veteran of D-Day, Hufford was serving as jeep driver for correspondents, occasionally including me. He said he would wait until I returned with the patrol. "Sure you're OK with this?" he asked. "Yeah," I answered, and he wished me luck.

Amid shouts of "Good luck, you guys," we set off at exactly 3:30 p.m.—15:30 hours. Our mission was to get to Rothenburg, about two miles behind the enemy's front lines, and negotiate the town's surrender. It was to be a mission of exactly three hours. If we were not back by 18:30 hours, the town would be bombarded by aerial and artillery fire. Just how the bombs were going to differentiate between us and the Germans was one of the subjects we would discuss along the way.

Years later, I would learn that our mission resulted from a last-minute conversation between U.S. Assistant Secretary of War John J. McCloy and General Jacob Devers, commanding the U.S. Sixth Army Group. McCloy had visited Devers's command post and reported in response to a letter from me:

> ... and it was there that [Devers] laid out the plan for the impending attack, which disclosed artillery preparations of considerable weight on the town of Rothenburg. I told him it was a shame at that late date in the war to destroy a city of such historical interest and beauty .... He immediately gave an order to effect its surrender and was quite determined about it.

At first there were nine of us in the patrol, all of us crammed into a jeep. Two guys from the Fourth Engineers were lying prone on the hood of the jeep and taking turns with a mine detector sweeping the road ahead of us. Two lieutenants were in the front, next to the driver, and four of us enlisted men, all privates first class, were in the back. The guy next to me was sitting against the spare tire and holding a long pole bearing a huge truce flag, about half of a white bed sheet.

"You don't have to use that detector now," one of the lieutenants shouted to the engineers as we were setting off, "but keep your eyes open; they might have put some in the road farther ahead." Then to the driver: "Take it a little slower."

The jeep crept along the macadam road for about a kilometer, and came to a halt near the edge of a hole that was almost as wide as the road. "Shell crater," somebody said. We got out and walked behind the engineer with the mine detector as he slowly swept a path to the crater. It was a shallow hole, and after we got out the jeep was able to get through it. We got back into the jeep and we were riding again.

As we came to a turn in the road, somebody said, "Who the hell's that up ahead?"

"It's Charlie Company," came the answer.

We reached and began to pass trough the two files of Charlie Company riflemen. With rifles slung over their shoulders, they were advancing at a slow pace, and at intervals of about ten yards along both sides of the road.

"Yo, where the hell you guys goin'?" one of them yelled.

"Rothenburg. Gonna get 'em to surrender."

"Well, good luck."

"Yeah, good luck, you guys," others joined in.

There was one more question before we passed on: "Hey Lichey, where the hell'd you get that sheet?"

"That's my secret," answered Herman Lichey, a tall guy from California. Having been born and raised in Germany, he spoke fluent German and was to be our translator in any negotiation for the surrender of the town.

A short time later we reached another hole in the road, much wider and deeper, too deep for the jeep to navigate. "Well, you guys might as well go back," one of the lieutenants said to the two engineers. He turned to the driver: "You can take them back with you."

That left six of us: First Lieutenant Noble V. Borders, Lousiville, Kentucky; First Lieutenant Edmund E. Austingen, Hammond, Indiana, and four privates: Herman Lichey, Glendale, California; Robert S. Grimm, Tower City, Pennsylvania; Peter Kick, Lansing, Illinois, and me, William M. Dwyer, Trenton, New Jersey.

We walked through the crater and up to the road surface again. Keck was carrying a heavy radio on his back. Next to him, Lieutenant Borders was holding the receiver to his ear. He was talking to battalion headquarters: "We are now proceeding on foot. We have passed two craters and are about 500 yards out in front of Charlie Company."

Austingen, the other lieutenant, said to us, "Keep your eyes peeled for mines."

Lichey was walking in the middle of the road, and we were spread out on both sides of him. Unwittingly we fell into step. "All we need now is a fife and drum and we're the

Spirit of Seventy-six," Lichey said. He was holding the truce flag high and enjoying his role.

We didn't stay in step for long.

"Hey, hear that?" somebody said.

Rifle fire, not far ahead of us; quite a bit of it.

"If we draw fire," Borders said, "there's nothing we can do but duck and try to get back."

The firefight seemed to grow louder with each step we took. Hmmm. Would the Germans be able to see the flag? Would they stop firing when they saw it?

There was a turn to the left in the road ahead. When we reached it, we could see some of our guys who were about 50 yards farther on. "Baker Company," somebody said. The Baker Company riflemen were off to the right of the road, firing at German positions on high ground straight ahead. And the Germans were firing back.

By the time we caught up with the Baker Company riflemen, those near the road had seen our flag and had stopped firing. But the other Baker guys, farther off to the right and presumably unable to see us, were still firing away. So were the Germans.

One of the riflemen lying face-down against a pile of debris was only a few yards from the road.

"Hey," he shouted, "what the hell are you guys doing here?"

"Going to Rothenburg, we hope," Lieutenant Borders said.

"What's up?"

"Gonna get 'em to surrender the town."

"Good deal. But watch out for that house on the right. It's full of Krauts; plenty of 'em."

"OK."

"Good luck!"

For a short time we walked in silence, except for the pounding of our GI boots on the macadam. Then somebody said, "The only thing is they might think it's a trick and we're sending back information on the radio."

"Well," said Borders, "don't touch the radio. And just keep walking natural."

"Yeah," said Austingen, "don't make any funny moves, anybody. Those sonsabitches probably have their sights on our bellies right now."

"Baker'll stop firing, but I don't know about the goddamn Krauts."

"Maybe they can't see the flag yet with all these bushes."

"What about the radio? If they fire, we'll have to break the radio right away."

"No, just change the channel."

"Hell, no, break it. They could find our channel easy. Break it."

Meanwhile even the Germans' firing from high ground had stopped.

We had almost reached the house full of Krauts, a large stone farmhouse built almost flush to the edge of the road. Uh-oh. Being on the extreme right, I would be walking within a yard or two of the house, right into the shadow it cast on the road. What the hell was I, a skinny 5 feet 9 inches, one of the Army's unlikeliest soldiers—I hadn't even been a Boy Scout—doing here?

Still, no firing from the house. Were they just waiting for a closer shot at us, or what? I could feel the eyes behind the dark windows peering at me as each step brought us closer to the house.

"Don't bunch up," Borders said. "Keep spread out, and don't touch that radio."

Going past the place, I faced straight ahead, but out of the corners of my eyes I was looking for a place to dive.

We came out of the shadow of the house and into the sunlight again. Now I could feel those eyes on the back of my neck. There was a turn in the road about 100 yards ahead, and I began to think we'd never reach it. But we did, and I exhaled deeply and felt a quiver down my back. There had been no dizzying swirl.

The afternoon sun was getting to me, and I was wishing I had left my sweater and field jacket behind. Ahead of us now there was elevated ground on each side of the road. On our left we could see tilled garden plots on a hillside sloping down to the road—and, just opposite us, an old farmer at work with a hoe! Right in the middle of no man's land. He paused, took a brief look at us, adjusted his straw hat, and resumed hoeing. He didn't wave, and neither did we.

On our left a little farther on, a lone figure crouched behind a spread of bushes. German artillery observer, we figured. Behind us the firefight came alive from both sides. "Intermission's over," somebody said. Ahead, everything was quiet.

"How about the major?" Borders said, referring to Frank Burk, commander of the First Battalion. "Out of the whole battalion he sends for me and says, Do I want to go? What the hell could I say?"

"Yeah," Austingen, the other lieutenant said, 'I want three volunteers—you, you and you.'"

Borders turned to Lichey. "Have you got it straight now, what you're going to say?"

"Yes, indeed," said Lichey, assuming a semi-serious tone. "We are representatives of our division commander. We bring you his offer to spare the city of Rothenburg from shelling and bombing if you agree not to defend it. We have been given three hours to get this message to you. If we haven't returned to our lines by 18:00 hours, the town will be bombed and shelled to the ground."

"That's it. We want the town and without a fight."

"You know," Austingen said, "this'll be something if it works."

For a while no one spoke. There was only the continuing sound of our GI boots against the macadam—klump, klump, klump, klump. Then "What the hell kind of place is Rothenburg?"

"It goes back to eleven hundred and something, and it has a wall around the whole place. Lots of art and . . . . Hey! Do you see what I see?"

"Yeah."

"Don't touch that radio. They might think it's a weapon."

"Just keep walking natural. Don't slow up."

Not far ahead of us, on the right, there was a large, yellowish farmhouse with a whitewashed stone wall jutting out to the road. It was twice as big as the house we had last passed, and this time there were signs that it was occupied. First a helmet appeared above the wall. Then two more. Uh-oh. Then three gun barrels, and they were pointed right at us.

"Just keep walking natural," Borders said.

"And keep spread out," Austingen said.

We were within forty yards of the place when the three bearing arms stepped out from the wall and on to the road. Slowly they started walking toward us. Two of them carried rifles, I noticed. The tallest one had a pistol, and he was so nervous the pistol shook in his hand. They kept walking and so did we. They didn't seem to know what to do next. Neither did we.

"*Halte!*"

It was the tall one with the pistol. We halted abruptly only a few yards from them. That pistol made us as nervous as he was.

They looked at one another. What next?

Lichey, holding the white flag, stepped forward and proceeded to explain our mission.

Meanwhile six or seven more Germans appeared from behind the wall. They formed a ring around us. I counted three whose collars bore the SS insignia—the mark of Heinrich Himmler's bully boys, the dreaded *Schutzstaffel.*

The six of us were escorted into the courtyard of the farmhouse. It was a cemented area measuring about 100 by 100 feet. The wall surrounded the entire yard. For what seemed like a long time we just stood near the back door of the farmhouse. Looking around the yard, I counted about forty of them, including seventeen with SS insignia. Most of them had stopped in their tracks when we entered and were still staring at us.

"See who some of these bastards are?" somebody whispered.

"Careful, they may compree English."

The tall one with the pistol indicated that he was going inside to get the *Kommandant.* Seconds later, a surly little lieutenant emerged, screaming at us.

"What's he saying, Lichey?"

"He wants to know why we are invading his country for the second time in his lifetime."

"Well," said Lieutenant Borders, "tell him we're not here to argue but to get to the officer in command of Rothenburg."

Lichey explained our mission as the lieutenant continued to glare at us. Then he went quickly back into the house. "He says he'll have to phone higher headquarters to find out what to do," Lichey said.

They put two armed guards on the six of us. They took our radio and set it aside. Then they searched us for weapons, and came up with only a pocket knife—made in Germany. With the guards' permission we moved into the shadow of a shed. We took off our helmets and sat on them. Some of the German soldiers came closer to us and started asking us questions, sometimes with their hands.

One of their first was about President Roosevelt, who had died a few days earlier. Roosevelt gut? Yes, we indicated, he was good. What president now? Truman. Gut? Yes, Truman was good.

At this point the surly lieutenant came out of the house and said he had called for transportation for us.

The lieutenant returned to the house, and the discussion continued. We were told they had walked more than 200 kilometers in the past three days, their food was not fit for a pig, and they no longer had beer or schnapps.

One of the Germans, who spoke English, said, "I hope this damn war is finished soon. I want to go home." At this point, two SS men, who had been standing nearby, came over holding rifles before them. One of them said, "The war will be finished when we have won it." They then ordered the

German soldiers away from us. *"Raus! Raus!"* they shouted and they were quickly obeyed.

Next a sergeant came out of the house bearing strips of white cloth. "They're going to blindfold us now," Lichey said. I stood up with the rest and felt a blindfold being adjusted over my nose and tied tightly at the back of my neck. For a time I was all alone. No one spoke. I wondered again about the swirl, but there was no swirl.

"Hey, Borders, you still here?"

"Yeah, how about you other guys?"

Our names were called out and we all responded. We kept it up as they were leading us off. "Still here?" "Yeah, still here."

What next? Was a firing squad lining up opposite that wall? "You guys still here?" Yes, we were, and on we went. One of the Germans was helping me keep my balance. Where the hell were they taking us?

I found myself being guided into some kind of vehicle; so were the others.

After sitting down, I was able to determine that I was in the left rear seat. Being the possessor of an oversized nose, I was, by tilting my head back, able to get a sliver of a view of our situation. In the rear seats of an open vehicle three of us were facing forward, and three of us were facing the rear, knees almost touching. Tilting my head backward again and pretending to scratch my nose, I discovered that in addition to the driver, there was an armed guard on each running board.

It turned out to be a long ride, with much starting, stopping, and changing of direction. Did the driver know what he was doing? Where the hell was he taking us?

Entering a town—was it Rothenburg?—I got partial glimpses of people standing at an intersection. Some of them were shouting and waving their fists. And spitting. I caught some of the spray on my chin.

"Hey," Lichey said, "you hear that? They're calling us '*Schweinhunden.*'"

"What the hell's that?"

"Pig-dogs."

"And here we are, trying to save their goddam town."

Time was running out, and we were wondering about that 18:30 deadline. We had apparently arrived at their goddam town, and, still blindfolded, we were being helped out of the vehicle. "You guys OK?" Yeah, we were OK. We were led down a long and steep path, into a building, and then up to what appeared to be the third floor of the building. Standing in a large, sunlit room, we were allowed to take off the blindfolds.

Now we were facing a major who was seated behind a large desk and surrounded by a dozen or more officers and a few noncoms. Glancing at his wristwatch, Borders said to Lichey, "Tell him what we want, and tell him we're running out of time. If we're not back at our CP [command post] in a half hour, we're *all* going to get bombarded. And tell him I've gotta use the radio to get an extension on the three hours."

The major listened attentively to Lichey then consulted with some of the officers surrounding him. A brief dialogue ensued, and after hearing the major out, Lichey said, "He says it's OK with him. He wants to give up the town and pull back. But he's not sure he can do it on his own. He needs an OK from higher up, and that'll take time."

Looking at his wristwatch, Borders said, "Tell him that in about a half hour this town will be leveled unless we're back at our CP. And tell him I gotta use the radio to get an extension. It'll take time for us to get back."

Our radio had been brought along, and "*Ja*," it was OK, and presently Borders was using it: "I have an urgent message for any Pine station, over." All eyes in the room were on him. There was no answer. "Can you hear me? Over." No answer. He tried and tried again as the minutes of the final half hour ticked away, but there was still no answer.

Turning to Lichey, Borders said, "Ask him how long it will take to get the final answer."

"He says maybe four hours. They've got trouble with communications."

"Four hours! That'd be 10 o'clock tonight. Too late. Tell him we can't wait that long. We've got to get back right away or we'll all be under heavy fire. Artillery's probably setting up right now."

Through Lichey, we received the major's assurance that he strongly favored surrendering Rothenburg and leaving the wounded—apparently there were many of them—in the town square. No need for a formal surrender. There could be a new meeting tomorrow morning and the surrender would be made.

"Tell him," Borders said as we prepared to leave, "we'll meet him in the morning if it's possible." Turning to us: "Now, let's get the hell out of here before it's too late."

Just before being blindfolded again, we put on our helmets and exchanged salutes with the Germans. The major responded with an American-style salute. Some of the others thrust their right arms forward, clicked their heels, and shouted, *"Heil Hitler!"* Just like in the movies, I thought. We stood in place as we were blindfolded again, and replaced our helmets.

Within a few minutes the six of us were back in the vehicle that brought us. Though blindfolded, Borders was able to use the radio and attempt to reach the battalion CP. There was still no answer, but he kept trying.

Just before we were led out of the vehicle and allowed to remove the blindfolds, he got through with his message: Hold the fire.

"Well," he said, exhaling deeply, "we don't have to sweat that any more."

The German driver and the non-com with him saluted our two officers smartly, made a roaring U-turn, and sped off.

Within five long minutes we were walking past the farmhouse where the SS men and others had been. A few elderly men and women were standing in front of the whitewashed wall. They waved and smiled diffidently. One woman was crying and wiping away tears. There were no soldiers in sight.

Farther on, Borders received some welcome news on the radio: "They're sending a jeep to meet you."

We were still wary of sniper fire, but after passing a bend in the road we spotted a GI lying near the road, holding an M-1 rifle. And then some other GIs.

We were safe at last.

"How'd you make out?" one of them shouted.

"OK."

"Good!"

Then we saw the jeep, and a lieutenant running toward us. He was carrying a bottle of liquor. "Nice going," he said, handing over the bottle. "They're putting all of you in for Silver Stars."

We took turns swigging it. It was Scotch that tasted like iodine diluted with water. But now it was champagne.

Officers and enlisted men were crowding around us—guys who'd been fighting the war, some of them since D-Day in Normandy—and slapping us on the back. "Good job!" "Nice going!"

We never did get Silver Stars (we were awarded Bronze Stars), but, for a rear-echelon soldier like me, at least, the looks they gave us were just as good as getting the Medal of Honor.

About six o'clock the next morning, troops of the First Battalion, Twelfth Regiment, Fourth Infantry Division, set off without artillery support and entered Rothenburg. They found some fifty wounded Germans who had been left in the town square. "As we moved into the city on one side," Lieutenant Borders noted in his journal, "the Krauts moved out the other side and into the woods beyond. Our battalion drew no fire from the city itself as we moved in, but there was sniper fire from the ground surrounding the city."

It was a most interesting and rather trying experience, but as far as I'm concerned, someone else may have my part of the honor of going on the next such mission.

For me, the experience at Rothenburg put me finally into the real war, and I no longer had conscience trouble about those risking their lives at the front. I had a good feeling knowing Bouton, Milton, and others knew I was there.

All except Leicester, who said it was only fair that I got some of the combat that he'd seen so much of. I just looked at him.

On April 20, 1945—four days after our patrol's venture into Rothenburg—the next such mission occurred: a three-member truce party from the First Battalion of the Fourth Division's 22nd Regiment went, under a white flag, into Crailsheim, a Bavarian city situated about 40 miles south of Rothenburg. In his history of the 22nd Regiment, Dr. William Boice, Chaplain of the regiment, reported:

> The First Battalion was ordered to take the town of Crailsheim, a city of perhaps some eight or ten thousand inhabitants. The Battalion drew up its ring of steel in preparation for the attack on the northern edge of the city and there stood fast while Lieutenant (Walter E.) Jones was ordered with two enlisted men to approach the city officials and arrange its surrender, by Lieutenant Colonel George Goforth, the Battalion Commander.
>
> This Lieutenant Jones immediately did, and upon approaching Crailsheim with an interpreter, he contacted the Burgomaster and gave to him the American terms for the surrender of the city. The terms had apparently been received and accepted when, without warning, the three American soldiers were shot in the back and killed.

When this information was given to Lieutenant Colonel Goforth, "he issued orders with tenseness and concealed fury, which communicated itself to every man in the battalion. Instead of ordering that the city be attacked, he called for artillery fire, and he personally adjusted the mortars, ordering them to fire white phosphorous and to burn every building in the city. These orders were carried out, with Colonel Goforth observing. If occasionally the smoke and flames blew away and a building was revealed still standing, the Colonel adjusted the mortars and soon the building was in flames. The city of Crailsheim will long have cause to remember a lieutenant named Jones and his funeral pyre."

The Germans paid heavily for the sniping. "It was a cowardly and needless gesture on the part of the Germans; it was a furious and just retaliation from a combat battalion which had learned to hate the treachery of a defeated enemy. A city died . . ."

Chaplain Boice added, "One of the things which Americans will never forget was the order requiring every German house to fly a white flag or be destroyed."

In *A Soldier's Journal,* published in 2003 by ibooks, David Rothbart, a sergeant who served in the 22nd Infantry Regiment, provides further information about Crailsheim and its residents. It is included in the November 1995 update to the entry he made in his journal on April 26, 1945:

> The Town of Crailsheim had once been home to Dr. Armin Ziegler and his family. Half a century after the event described in this entry, Dr. Ziegler undertook an investigation that corrected the record of what happened on April 20, 1945. Both my entry, and the memoir of our regimental Chaplain Dr. William Boice, indicated that the citizens of Crailsheim had acted in a dishonorable fashion. Dr. Ziegler obtained full documentation from United States Official Army records that proves otherwise. Lt. Walter E. Jones was shot not in the back but in the throat. No white flags of surrender were displayed, because the residents were forbidden to do so by diehard German SS troops, who threatened death to anyone who defied their orders. I heartily welcome this new information. No sane person would willingly cause more death and destruction when the war was so near the end.

Dachau

Devastating scenes of Dachau

On the afternoon of April 31, 1945, along with other members of the Fourth Infantry Division, I was given a tour of Dachau, the German concentration camp where tens of thousands of prisoners perished. Two days earlier, some prisoners there had been liberated by Allied troops.

Toward the end of the war, the German army was retreating haphazardly in the face of vastly superior Allied forces. One of the places, overrun during this final rout, was the infamous prison camp at Dachau.

At the time it was liberated, one sunny spring day in 1945, Dachau presented some unbelievable sights both inside and outside its walls. Outside, on a railroad siding near the main entrance, there was a line of boxcars—38 of them, if my recollection is accurate—each loaded to the top with dead men: 38 boxed piles of emaciated bodies, some with arms reaching skyward, some seemingly frozen in the act of crawling over a boxcar wall. It was an appalling sight even for American infantrymen who had been living with death since D-Day in Normandy: the sunken cheeks, the shaven heads, the dark sockets that once had been eyes, the limp, grotesquely twisted bodies clad in prison uniforms that looked like striped pajamas . . .

Inside the prison camp there were more of the dead and some about to die. The SS prison guards had fled. The prisoners strong enough to walk and talk were escorting newly arrived American infantrymen about the place.

One of the prisoners, a French priest, pointed to bloodstains on a paved area near the main entrance. Right there, he said, one of the SS guards had been beaten down by a group of liberated prisoners and then literally torn apart.

Dachau!

So this was where it happened, I thought, as I walked about the place, scarcely believing what I saw and smelled. So here it was that the innocents were slaughtered. Here were the ovens, the shower rooms. Already *Dachau* had become a dirty word.

Outside, just across the street from one of the prison walls, the rear wall, as I recall, there was a cluster of neat, lookalike houses. Here, I learned, had lived the SS prison guards and their families. The SS men were gone now, but some of their wives and children, it could be seen, were still living in these little homes.

It was a strange sight: on one side of the street, life; on the other, death. For how many long years had it been so? Children—tanned, healthy-looking kids—were at play, and mothers were busy with household chores on one side of the street; on the other, behind that wall, pale and shrunken human beings were on their deathbeds.

How did one feel, I got to wondering, living a family life in a sun-speckled house just across the way from a human slaughterhouse? How had these wives and mothers—healthy looking, neatly dressed women—adjusted to the butchery carried out for years right under their noses? Surely they knew what their husbands' work had been, *nicht?* How had they rationalized it? Had they ever objected or protested?

With such questions in mind, and accompanied by a German-speaking GI, I decided to approach some of the women. Not entirely out of curiosity; I was a correspondent for *Stars and Stripes*, (a lowly divisional correspondent, indeed, but assigned to an outstanding division, the 4th), and I thought the women's answers would make a likely story for the paper. (Not so, as things turned out.)

But their answers come to mind these days as innocent humans are daily blown to bits by high-altitude American bombing in Cambodia with no mass protest. What could they have done? The women of Dachau asked. How could one have stopped it? What does one do in wartime but follow orders, *nicht?* How could one object or protest without risking one's life and the lives of their loved ones?

One of the women, I recall, said that her best friend had been executed for a remark made about slave labor. Some of the others cited similar examples of "crime" and punishment under Nazi rule. What, indeed, was one to do?

(The following are excerpts from a letter, signed by William M. Dwyer, to New Jersey's U.S. Senators, Clifford P. Case and Harrison A. Williams.)

**Bombs on Cambodia,
You and I and the Women of Dachau,**
The Evening Times, Trenton, New Jersey, May 16, 1973

Looking to the future, I find myself wondering these days what answers you and I will give when our grandchildren raise the kind of questions asked of those SS wives. Will we be able to live with the answers we give? The "enemy" did bad things, too; the bombing was justifiable and necessary, just as the administration spokesmen said it was. Will this sort of rationalization hold up in the eyes of our young ones? Will they be inclined to forgive us if we point out how occupied we were with Watergate and other scandals? I wonder.

But is our present position analogous to that of the women of Dachau? I think it is. Today's news coverage and communications networks being what they are, we are just as close to the slaughter being carried out in Cambodia as those women were to the slaughter in Dachau prison. It is happening right under our noses; we can see no boxcars full of corpses, but we can easily visualize the gory results of what American pilots are doing halfway around the globe.

There is, however, a basic difference. Unlike the women of Dachau, we Americans can protest our country's barbaric acts without fear of punishment. As a people we can, if only we will, put enough pressure on the Commander-in-Chief to force a halt of the aerial slaughter. (God knows the President's policy in Cambodia no more reflects the will of most Americans than Watergate reflects that of the vast majority of Republicans.) And you, as an influential and respected member of the Senate long devoted to the struggle for peace, can do much more in this respect than any of us back home can do. You and the other responsible members of the Senate have it within your power to concur in the Congressional vote on Cambodia, to put an end to the savagery. And quickly.

The choice, it seems to me, is clear, especially when one thinks of those questions our grandchildren are going to ask.

Southern Germany was swarming with liberated inmates of concentration camps and "slave laborers," as the members of forced labor units were usually called. Many of them came as close as they could to headquarters of the Fourth Infantry Division. They were hungry, some emaciated, and they took food wherever they could find it, as a gift from some of the American GIs or from the garbage cans into which the GIs emptied out their mess kits following a meal.

It was a time of great confusion, especially for the victims of the Nazis who had been taken from their homes either in Germany or one of the Nazi-invaded countries. American army trucks were being used to transport the liberated men and women on the first leg of their long journeys home.

One of the things I remember most vividly from this time was the departure of a group of some 20 or more slave laborers from a village in southern Germany. The slaves were standing there in a sort of village square, and they were crying. So were the members of the farm families the slaves had worked for. What was this? Another Fourth Division GI and I wondered as we took in the scene. The slaves were, as they awaited their turn to get on the Army trucks, embracing the Germans whose farms they had worked. The slaves and the Germans were all crying, all promising to keep in touch, all saying that some day they would meet again.

Unbelievable. Especially so in the context of what we had been seeing. But there it was—real feelings of friendship, of love, between the masters and the slaves. Not all of the Germans had acted like hardened Nazis.

End of the War

Lucky me on R&R in Nice, May 1945

Nice, France

When the War was declared over, my name was picked out of a hat and I spent a month in Nice sometimes sleeping happily under a gaming table.

A couple months later we were back home.

It was our first night back in the States, a night in July 1945. With thousands of other members of the US Fourth

Infantry Division, Leicester Hemingway and I had landed in New York early that morning after crossing the Atlantic on a ship called the *USS Hermitage.*

The war in Europe was over. The Fourth Division had been through five campaigns. We were proud of the division's record, but we were not exactly looking forward to any additions to that record. As things stood, we were, after a 30-day furlough, scheduled to go on to the Pacific and there become part of a force invading Japan. (Luckily for us, VJ Day would cancel that trip.)

On our first day back from Europe we found ourselves in a place called Camp Shanks. It had been our point of departure for Europe two years earlier. It was, as I recall, about a 25-minute bus ride out of Manhattan.

That night, our first in the States, Leicester (Call me Hank) Hemingway and I, both now elevated to private first class, sneaked out of Shanks. There were strict orders to remain in camp that night, but what the hell could they do to us?—and thumbed our way to Manhattan. Although we were veterans with a couple of years of service in England, France, Belgium, Luxembourg and Germany, we must have looked like a couple of newly inducted yahoos. That afternoon we'd been issued new khakis that didn't fit very well. My size 16 neck was surrounded by a size 18 shirt collar. My new ballooning trousers fit me about as well as those pants used to fit "Cheese and Crackers" Fagan on the burlesque circuit.

But, what the hell! We were back home, and things were looking up. Tonight we wouldn't even mention the possibility of going to Japan. Tonight we'd celebrate. Leicester had had an encouraging word or two from a publisher about a war novel he'd been writing for the past year. And I'd just heard from my agent, Bertha Klausner. She'd sold my first-person story to *Liberty* about the surrender of Rothenburg on the Tauber, Germany.

Our first stop was a crowded little bar in the east Fifties. There, over a beer or two, Leicester told me how he was going to make it, by God, as a writer, just as his elder brother Ernest had made it. And I was going to make it, too. (A few weeks later *Liberty* went out of business before my piece could be published.)

But what the hell were we doing in a crummy little bar like this on our first night back? After all those months of dreaming about being back in the States, wasn't there a more appropriate place?

There was indeed, it turned out. We were only a short walk from Sherman Billingsley's wonderful Stork Club, the place that Walter Winchell was always touting in his column. What better place for the first night back in the land of the free?

But, we presently learned, the guy at the door of the Stork Club had other ideas. He took one look at us and turned us down. No tables available. But what about the bar? we asked. It was possible to get a glimpse of the bar and to see that it wasn't fully occupied. But the doorman, taking another look at our ill-fitting khakis, rolled his eyes toward the ceiling, and once more said "No."

And who in this cockeyed world should come striding along at just that moment but Lucille Ball, the actress (later of *I Love Lucy* fame) sporting the orangest hair I've ever seen? She was accompanied by an older woman. Her agent, we later learned.

"What's the trouble?" she asked. "What's going on here?"

We explained that all we wanted to do was have a beer or two but the guy wouldn't let us in. No room.

"No room!" Miss Ball said to the guy on the door. "What do you mean no room? Why don't you give them the table I just left?"

And so forth. Miss Ball did her best, but it wasn't good enough. No mere soldiers were getting into the Stork Club that night. "Sorry fellas," said Miss Ball, exiting with a smile and a shrug. "I'd ask you to come along and have a drink with me, but I'm behind schedule already. Good luck to you."

Then, with a final sneer at the guy blocking our way, she departed. I can still see her striding off into the night.

(See the anthology of columns at the end for more on Leicester Hemingway.)

Letter from Camp Butner to Jim Faber
not too long after the Lucy incident.

(Jim Faber was the childhood friend who threw Bill's bathing suit away while skinny dipping in the canal at the Crossing causing Bill to run all the way down the River Road "bare-assed naked.")

Dear Jim,

Your postcard came through the other day just before I packed my duffle bag and dragged my weary ass to Dix. I reported back on the 14^{th,} the day after the war ended. I considered a week of AWOL but decided to return on time because I didn't want to foul up any possible chance for discharge.

We stayed at Dix a few hours then headed here where we learn we're still going to go through a training program, then head for the Pacific (that is, all those with fewer than 75 pts). If a certain general order comes out, I'll have 73 points which, under present plans, will be good for a sojourn in the Orient. Because it's in the future and many changes can come about in the next few weeks, I haven't bothered to become pissed off yet.

It was good to hear you're at the Sorbonne. I was going to try to take such a course but we were alerted for the States before enrollment started. Eight weeks in that place should give you enough stimulation for a life time.

It is a rare experience, getting back to the States. You will probably have the same feelings I had. At first everything and almost everybody seems silly. Later, some of the people seem to make sense and others appear even sillier and in many cases more callous.

The Eastern Aircraft crowd for example (Bill had worked there before the war editing their house letter)—not all of them but many of them. When the peace rumors became red hot I heard them say, "I hope the Japs hold out till Thursday, 'cause then we'll get Friday, Saturday and Sunday off." To many, VJ Day means now they can't be drafted; now they can say "Fill 'er up" and buy all the meat and silk stockings they need.

It makes you slightly sick to hear some of them but there isn't any point in being righteous and offended. So you do your best to ignore them—though it is sometimes difficult.

At first being in Trenton was like visiting a strange city. Except for the family and a few others, I didn't seem to know anybody. Even Conte's (a local bar) was strange and heavy with gamblers and war wives on the make.

But after a while you begin to feel at home and with the arrival of McCardell (also on 30-day leave) and of course, Brown (who came down from Rochester), and Joe Feehan, and several others, you begin to have a good time. All in all, it was a good furlough.

When do you think you'll be home? And out? The Army certainly hates to let the guys go, even the old guys. There are beaucoup PO'd guys here and I can imagine how you feel. "Fine thing for a young fellow," I see they persist in saying.

Last week I received some pleasant news from my agent, which said that "Liberty" had bought one of my stories for $400. Don't have the check yet but it's supposed to be on the way. The sale is very encouraging and probably rescued me from a rejection slip complex. I have several other stories I'm now sweating out.

And that's about all. Hope you get home soon although I know how slow the Army can be.

Best of luck and keep it in your pants,
Bill

It was a hot afternoon in August when I finally walked up the steps for good to 572 Bellevue Avenue. Before I could call through the screened door they were all out there: Helen, who'd received the telegram from the War Department when Ed died; Nan, married to a flier; my little sister Del, Mom still with her apron on, and Pop, who'd taken off from work. We fell on each other, laughing and crying as we went into the house. There was the aroma of good home cooking coming from the kitchen and a happy, noisy energy I hadn't felt in a long time.

I was home.

It was so familiar yet so different. Two and a half years had passed since I had lived here. Gran'mom was gone. My brother Ed buried thousands of miles away in Hawaii's military cemetery, the Punchbowl. Eddie Mathews up the street killed in action, my brother-in-law Ed Schmierer's brother, Jack, also dead. Loss had become part of the American fabric. This was long before Helen's descent into schizophrenia and her eventual suicide, Del's sudden death from an aneurysm, Nan's widowhood at age 40, and my divorce and remarriage, causing a priest from St. Joe's to promise my mother he would pray for my death so that I wouldn't be caught in eternal purgatory.

But on that day in 1945 there was a bright future looming up ahead; there was hope and laughter and peace at last.

* * *

I went on to a long career as a journalist, writing columns and features for *The Trenton Times*, contributing to *The New York Times, The Herald Tribune, Commonweal, Coronet,* and

New Jersey Monthly. I was press secretary to New Jersey's Governor, Richard J. Hughes, during the summit conference between President Lyndon B. Johnson and Premier Alexei Kosygin at Hollybush on the campus of Glassboro State College, and I was with Hughes during the turbulent Newark riots in the 60s. For a while I ran a writers' workshop in the heart of Trenton to engage young blacks and Hispanics in the craft and arranged jobs for them at local papers if they showed promise. I also wrote a couple of books, most recently, *The Day Is Ours!,* about how a ragged rebel army stood the storm and saved the American Revolution, published by Viking.

At the age of 53, I became a father for the first and only time when my second wife, Marge, gave birth to our daughter Suzy, who very easily became the sunshine of our lives.

Did I ever regain my faith?, you may ask. Not in any formal way. As my life progressed I very easily fell into the religion of Lincoln, who, when asked what his was, answered simply, "When I do good, I feel good. When I do bad, I feel bad. That's my religion."

The war brought together a bunch of regular guys, people you saw in towns every day, dealt with in stores, restaurants, banks and professions all across America. Men who weren't really well prepared for combat but, with only basic training, gave it their all.

We were part of a greater picture, bigger than our home towns and bigger than our individual pursuits. And because of that, World War II—despite the horror and my huge personal loss (the death of my only brother, my best friend, and the one who knew me better than anyone ever would again)—was the experience that opened up the world to me and in so doing became the defining moment of my life.

PART III

Anthology of Selected Columns and Profiles

Dorothy Commins, People You Meet Along the Way,
Trenton Times, early 1960's

Back in the 1960s, my wife Marge and I were once invited to dine at the home of the man who mowed our lawn for six dollars a pop. He was from the isle of Ischia in the Gulf of Naples where he had been a teacher, but here in America he did not have the credentials and worked as a maintenance man supplementing his income by cutting grass on weekends. He would come with his young son as helper and at break time they would sit at our redwood picnic table way back under the trees and cool off with a jug of home made muscatel.

On this particular evening we found ourselves seated at the dinner table with five or six others whose lawns he mowed. I introduced myself and Marge to the person sitting next to me, a white-haired woman in her sixties, and she responded, "I am Mrs. Commins."

"Any relation to the great Saxe Commins?"

"He was my husband."

Thus began a friendship with one of the most interesting persons we have ever known. Dorothy Commins's late husband Saxe was, in the words of Irwin Shaw, "the best editor I have ever worked with and very likely the best editor in America in the twentieth century." Among the writers whom he edited—and influenced and befriended—were Eugene O'Neill, William Faulkner, Sinclair Lewis, Theodore Dreiser, James Michener, W. H. Auden, William Carlos Williams and Isak Dineson.

Saxe Commins died in 1958 after working as senior editor at Random House for a quarter of a century. Dorothy died almost 30 years later. Whenever I think of her, I remember some of the stories she told, and often it's one she told one evening during dinner at her home in Princeton about James and Nora Joyce.

The Comminses were in Paris in 1928, as I recall, a short time after they were married. One afternoon at a tea hosted by a couple they knew, Mrs. Commins found herself conversing with Nora Joyce and some other women. James Joyce's "Ulysses" was banned in America but it was the talk of Paris.

"You must be very proud of your husband, he has such a brilliant mind," Mrs. Commins said to Mrs. Joyce.

"Yes," she said, "but such a dirty one."

Another story Mrs. Commins told to us that wonderful evening at our grass cutter's house, between the many courses of fine Italian food, was the story of Brownie, a longshoreman who had been brought down to the Commins home in Princeton as an expert in the jargon used on the New York docks. Also spending the weekend was Budd

Schulberg. They were at work on a film script of "On the Waterfront."

In the course of the visit it was learned that Brownie managed to squirrel away a side of beef or two from the many crates of goodies coming in daily from Argentina. Where did he store it? In the confessional at the local Catholic church nearby.

After dinner while the men worked, Mrs. Commins went to Brownie's room to turn down the covers of his bed and was struck by the exquisite silk Sulka pajamas and robe on the bed. Elegant toilet articles were also displayed in a dark green brocaded case. It wasn't hard to guess where they had come from.

In her book "What is an Editor?" published by the University of Chicago Press, Dorothy Commins recalls "It was past midnight, and we had all turned in, when I heard a tip-toeing down the hall. Thinking that Budd or Brownie was in need of something, I quickly slipped into a robe and stepped into the hall. There I saw Brownie fishing into the pocket of his coat which was hanging in the hall closet.

"'Brownie, are you all right?'"

"'Yeah, lady, this is what I want,' and with that he showed me a leather case, somewhat larger than a key case. When he opened it, there rested a string of rosary beads on a colored lithograph of the Madonna. All Brownie said was, 'I can't get to sleep without it. I always put it under my pillow.'"

Charles S. Gilpin, The Original 'Emperor Jones,'
Trenton Evening Times, May 8, 1963

It was a dull evening in the city room of the *Trenton State Gazette*. No news wasn't good news when you were trying to put together a paper for the next morning.

Hoping for a local story for Page One, the managing editor spoke to one of his best reporters.

"Anything good?"

"Not a thing," the reporter said, "not even any obits, except one guy that died out in Eldridge Park."

Although few people knew it, the "guy" who died that day—May 6, 1930—was a big story.

He was a Negro named Charles Sidney Gilpin. At a time when a Negro's chances for theatrical success were even more limited than they are today, he had become an all-time great of the American stage.

Gilpin, who had once earned more than $1,000 a week in Hollywood, died at the age of 51 in a modest home at 21 Emden Avenue just 33 years ago yesterday. He had spent part of his boyhood in the Lambertville area, and had lived his last four years in Lawrence Township, first on Eggerts Crossing Road and finally in Eldridge Park. His widow, Alma Bynum Gilpin, still lives there.

Gilpin had achieved his greatest success in 1920—at the age of 42—when he created the title role of Eugene O'Neill's "Emperor Jones." A big hit, it was brought from Greenwich Village (the Provincetown Playhouse) to Broadway for a long run.

For once the critics agreed:

In the *New York Times*, Alexander Wollcott said this of Gilpin: "they have acquired an actor, one who has it in him to invoke the pity and terror and the indescribable foreboding which are part of the secret of Emperor Jones."

Kenneth MacGowan in the *Globe*: "Gilpin's is a sustained and splendid piece of acting. The moment when he raises his naked body against the moonlit sky, beyond the edge of the jungle, and prays, is such a dark lyric of the flesh, such a cry of the primitive being, as I have never seen in the theater."

He first made Broadway in 1919 when he played the Rev. William Custis in John Drinkwater's "Abraham Lincoln." After that he was Brutus Jones, a part for which he had to compete with some of the day's leading white actors.

He was forced to retire in 1926 when he lost his booming voice. He did appear occasionally after that, but never with the success of his earlier days.

He is generally acknowledged to be America's first "serious" Negro actor, and many say he was the greatest. For his performance as Emperor Jones, the Drama League named him one of the ten persons who, in 1920, had contributed the most to the theater.

As the first Negro to be so honored, he was at first reluctant to attend the Drama League dinner. He thought he might not be welcome. But he went, and his speech was the hit of the evening.

> I like to keep the footlights between me and the public. I don't go in much for hobnobbing . . . I have my own little circle of friends and I love them. I live quietly in Harlem where I belong. I am really a race man, a Negro, and proud of being one, proud of the

progress the Negroes have made in the time and with the opportunity they have had.

If I can give anyone pleasure with my acting, I am happy.

Born in Richmond, in 1878, Gilpin was the youngest of 14 children. He attended a Catholic school there where a Sister Jerome recognized his talent and planted the idea of becoming an actor.

One of the few who became friendly with the Negro actor was a white man, James Salt of 722 Cherry Tree Lane, Eldridge Park, who said recently:

Charles Gilpin was a great singer, a great actor and a great man. He was the first Negro to play down South. They warned him he'd have trouble, but he went anyway and he made a big hit.

We used to go fishing together. He once gave me a German-made fishing reel. I remember once he got a telegram from the colored boxer, Jack Johnson saying: 'Charles, don't bet on me. If I win I'll never come out of the ring alive.' It was Johnson's fight with Jess Willard and Johnson lost.

Gilpin was buried in Lambertville 33 years ago this week. But that was not his final resting place. When word of his death reached Harlem, his friends insisted upon his removal to the place where he was beloved and best known. A few days later, hundreds of his admirers gathered for another funeral service, and re-interment, in Woodlawn Cemetery, Harlem.

Breakfast at the White House,
The Trenton Times, 1970

One morning I was home putting out the garbage and running late for work when The Call came.

Answer it and you'll be late for your first appointment. Ignore it and sure as hell it's your agent telling you Harper and Row has offered a $50,000 advance for another book idea but that contract has to be signed today. An earlier call that I answered had been the Dandy Diaper Service.

You answer it, a bit breathlessly, to show that the call has interrupted you at a busy time "Hello."

"Good morning, is this Mr. Dwyer?" asked a feminine voice with a heavy southern accent.

"Yes, it is."

"Mr. Dwyer, this is the wah house calling."

"The what?"

"The wah house."

"The White House?" Can this be a joke? Johnson had chosen not to run again because of the anti-Vietnam sentiment. So, who in the Nixon white house would be calling me? And why?

"Yes," the lilting voice on the 'phone continues, "The President would like you and Mrs. Dwyer to join him at the Wah House for a religious ceremony this Sunday."

The President! My god, or is this my buddy Jim Miller putting me on.

If so, he's doing a good job, for the voice is going on, matter-of-factly, and quite pleasantly, with the details: "The service will begin at 10:15 this Sunday morning in the East Room of the White House and it will be conducted by Doctor Billy Graham. Thirty-six members of the glee club of Bucknell University will provide the music and . . ."

Hey, it begins to occur to you, this really **is** the White House. But how come . . .

" . . . and the President would be honored," the Southern belle continues, "to have you and Mrs. Dwyer as his guests."

On the sprightly voice goes, and, with your head spinning just a little you find yourself explaining to Dorothy Johnson of the White House that Marge, who is expecting and beginning to show quite a bit, is not up to a trip to Washington, although she is feeling fine, and just about at this point it occurs to you that perhaps you are supplying more details than the White House needs at 9:30 of a Tuesday morning, and you say that as a matter of fact you'll be in Washington anyway over the coming weekend to attend the Gridiron Club dinner at the Statler Hilton. You accept with pleasure.

Aha! The reason for the mysterious call from the Wah House emerges: They're inviting people who'll be at the Gridiron Club dinner Saturday night. And through the generosity of Fletcher Knebel, a longtime member of the club, you're an invited guest. So that's it.

You've meanwhile mumbled your goodbye and thanks to the White House and you're putting out the rest of the garbage—where the hell does it all come from anyway?—and as you do you go into a couple of Charleston dance steps and neighbor Rhody Hall, backing out of his driveway across the street, gives you a what-the-hell's-got-into-him look but he waves and smiles as he drives away and how come he didn't stop so you could have said in a very calm voice that you'd just been invited to the White House but then you could tell him about it later anyway.

And so, five days later, on a sunny Sunday morning, you find yourself walking up the curved driveway that leads to the main entrance of the White House. With Polly Meara, no less, beautiful Polly Jamieson Meara, of Trenton, New Jersey, walking at your side. (Polly and husband Ed had been at the Gridiron dinner but not invited to White House.)

Just inside the gate, a man with a clipboard had stopped you and said,

"Mister . . . ?"

"Mr. Dwyer," you'd said, "Mr. and Mrs. Dwyer, as a matter of fact."

"But . . ." he'd said looking again at the sheets on his clipboard. "It only just says, Mr. Dwyer."

"Oh, yes, but Mrs. Dwyer was feeling much better and decided to come . . ."

"Hmmm."

It was at this moment that Polly Meara, her feminine instincts bubbling, took your arm. Took it possessively, and looked the man with the clipboard straight in the eye.

"Okay," he said, and the two of you passed on, arm in arm, and looked at the flowers that lined the way, at the endless line of black limousines, at the tennis court way down there at the edge of the lawn, and you observed it was a nice day to be visiting the White House, and wasn't that man standing over there listening to his wife Attorney General Mitchell?

Inside, there's a display of the works of Andrew Wyeth. Beautiful stuff, including Christina's World and all the rest of Wyeth's great ones.

And suddenly there you are, March 15, 1970, in the East Room of the White House, sipping freshly squeezed orange juice and taking in the scene:

The choir is singing and, isn't that Walter Cronkite over there?

President Nixon is shaking hands and exchanging remarks with an endless line of visitors. Next to him, Billy Graham—correction, Doctor Billy Graham—looking like an off-duty Seaside Heights lifeguard tall, bronzed, smiling, his hair bleached by the sun. And next to Dr. Graham, the President's wife, Pat Nixon, an anxious smile frozen on her face. A finely chiseled face, but somehow softer and far more attractive than it appears in print. She's wearing a golden yellow suit; a Chanel suit, according to a lady nearby, and her hair is teased into champagne swirls and puffs.

"I never realized Mrs. Nixon was so tiny," says the woman blocking the path to the coffee table. "My, isn't she tiny?" another voice agrees.

You take another look. Yes, she is. About the size of your sister Nan, five-two or so, but much thinner—92 pounds at the most. And you can tell that she'll be glad when the handshaking and small talk are finished; there's a bit of anxiety and fatigue in that frozen smile. In sharp contrast to the President, who is relaxed and attentive to the crowd.

During the service you observe Billy Graham saying, "Jesus Christ is in this room here and now." And that every so many rows there is a black person.

What are they going to do, invite, Sunday morning by Sunday morning, everybody in the country down for hymns and biscuits and pretty soon nobody'll oppose anything they do?

What would Granma Larkin say, all these Protestants—not to mention Aunt Maggie, who was sure you'd never get to heaven if you went to a Protestant service?

Writing at Home,
Trenton Times, March 7, 1971

One of the joys of writing a column at home is that you are able . . . whoops, there goes the telephone.

WOMAN AT DOOR: Hello, I'm Mrs. Smith.

YOU: Hello, Mrs. Smith.

WOMAN: And this is my friend, Mrs. Jones.

YOU: Hello, Mrs. Jones. Are you new neighbors or . . .

MRS. SMITH: No, we're from Jehovah's Witnesses.

YOU: Oh.

MRS. SMITH: We'd like to talk to you about the harmony of the gospels.

YOU: Huh?

MRS. JONES: And about how you can learn from the miracles of Jesus.

YOU: Well, it's kind of a bad time. I have this deadline I'm trying to meet. And my wife is upstairs feeding the baby.

MRS. SMITH: Perhaps we may come back another time?

YOU: Well, we've got this new baby, and things are kind of hectic here.

MRS. JONES: Perhaps you would enjoy reading the word of God in this copy of *The Watchtower*. . . .

MRS. SMITH: And please take this. It's our program for Kingdom Hall in Trenton with a word about your ancestors—were they men or apes?

Some minutes later you're back at the typewriter wondering about your ancestors and where you were when the doorbell sounded. Oh, yes:

One of the joys of writing a column at home is that you are able . . .

Whoops, there goes the telephone.

It's another insurance man. Congratulations on the birth of your daughter. Thanks. Have you given any thought to what might happen to her if SOMETHING were to happen to you? And so forth, for ten minutes.

Is that the baby crying? Yes it is. Hey, Marge, the baby is crying. What? Is it a hungry cry? How do I know? The baby is crying, period.

A devastating line occurs to you. Look, Marge, how about if you feed the baby and I'll watch "As the World Turns," until you finish and then I'll tell you what you've missed . . . .

No, that would be nasty. Besides, the baby seems to have stopped crying.

There goes the phone again. It's nephew Kerry, calling from the principal's office of the Lawrence Intermediate School. He's missed his bus and can you come and pick him up? How come he missed his bus? Well, he was playing basketball. And in the basketball game he accidentally pushed a kid and the kid kicked him in the wrist, his bad wrist from the fight with Sam the other day, and they both got kicked out of the game and now five friends of the kid that kicked him in the wrist are waiting to beat him up if he comes out of the principal's office.

You drop everything and spend a half hour picking Kerry up at school and trying to sort out what happened in the basketball game and how come kids can terrorize a kid that's in the principal's office. But you finally give up and you tell

Kerry, Yes, he can go out and play and stay out until you finish this column.

One of the joys of writing a column at home is that you are able to set your own . . .

Damn! The doorbell and Marge is upstairs feeding the baby. Who's keeping an eye on "As the World Turns?" Will Lisa and Bob ever get it all together? Will Penny ever find happiness?

It's the DyDee serviceman at the door—$3.55 for 80 more diapers. And the dirty ones? Oh, yes, the dirty ones. You go upstairs and get the hamper with the dirty ones. It weighs just short of a ton, but you somehow manage to get it to the door without suffering a hernia. Then upstairs with 80 new diapers—enough, you hope, to get Suzanna, now six weeks old, through another week. Kitchy-coo with Suzanna for a minute or two, what a charming young lady, and then back to the typewriter, but this time the telephone rings before you even get started.

It's Mr. Sweeney from the *Trentonian* . . . *Trentonian!* Returning Kerry's call. No, you tell Mr. Sweeney, Kerry's out playing somewhere. He'll be back around five o'clock. Okay, back to work.

Another knock from a magazine salesman. He'll receive 100 votes if you subscribe to one magazine, but if you subscribe to three he'll get all kinds of bonus points.

Seven or eight somewhat unpleasant minutes later, you're en route to the typewriter but you find Kerry in your path.

KERRY: Guess what.

YOU: WHAT?

KERRY: I'm going into the newspaper business.

YOU: Yeah?

KERRY: Yeah. You know that corner where the Jack and Jill store is? Tomorrow morning I'm going to start selling papers there.

YOU: Yeah?

KERRY: Yeah, Mr. Sweeney just called and they're going to deliver 20 papers here beginning tomorrow morning. I make four cents every paper I sell.

YOU: Yeah?

KERRY: Yeah, and all you have to do is call me at five o'clock in the morning.

YOU: Yeah?

Kerry: Yeah.

YOU: You mean to tell me that in the dark of night somebody's going to drop 20 *Trentonians* on my lawn, and I'm going to have to get you up at five o'clock in the morning to go out on the corner in the cold and the dark, to work for two hours to make, let's see 80 cents if you sell them all . . . .

KERRY: That's the general idea.

Three phone calls and two knocks at the door later, you're staring at the keys of your typewriter and wondering how you ever got into the column business anyway and Suzanna is crying a really hungry cry and Kerry is asking for help with his math homework and Marge is wondering if you've filled out your income tax for 1970 and if you'd mind going down to the drugstore for some Similac.

And once more the telephone rings. It's Jim Miller. He wants to know if you're interested in some tennis at the Mercer County Center.

Look, you tell Jim Miller, you've got this column to finish and that goddam dog from next door is on the loose again and Kerry's got to be called at 5 A.M. tomorrow to go out and sell *Trentonians*, and Suzanna's starting to cry, and you've got to get down to the drugstore to get some Similac, and you've got this thing from Jehovah's Witnesses about whether your ancestors were men or apes.

And then you decide the hell with all this nonsense. When will there be a better time to go play a couple of sets with good old Jim Miller? So you say you'll see him there in 30 minutes.

Hugh Kahler, A Reformed Second-rater Finds Success as a Writer,
The Trenton Times, Spring 1973

"It was a wonderful life," Hugh Kahler (1883-1969) told me during an interview in the spring of 1963. "We were living the good life at a place called Southern Pines, North Carolina—my wife Louise, our daughter Kingsley, and I. We played golf almost every day. We rode horses with our fox-hunting neighbors, who couldn't have been more congenial—writers like Struthers Burt and James Boyd and their wives, and visitors like John Galsworthy, and people who'd followed us down from Princeton.

"It was the summer of 1916, and I was writing something like a million words a year and selling them for something like a penny apiece, all under pen names, to the pulps, mostly those of *Street and Smith.* Now and then I sold a story to *Smart Set* that I felt I could sign with my own name.

"It was a good life, I thought, and I was pretty happy about living it. To be sure, Louise kept urging me to try my hand at something better than the pseudonymous stories that paid our bills. And sometimes I would fumble at a beginning, but I was secretly afraid I might lose my confidence if I ran into a rejection from *Collier's,* or even—supposing I dared to fly so high—the *Saturday Evening Post.* As a result I never managed to finish one of those ambitious stories. It was easier and safer to keep on selling hasty-pudding fiction to the pulpwoods.

"And then, on one of those peculiarly lovely November days that happen only to the North Carolina pinelands, Louise and I were coming home from a drive down-state. And as we rode through that golden afternoon my heart was high.

"I started to make a kind of Anthem about what had happened to me. Here I was, the boy who had worked on a farm for fifty cents a day, who had waded through ankle-deep slush to a dismal red-brick school during endless Buffalo winters. Only a little while ago I'd been commuting six days a week to a heart-breaking job in New York. And now, here I was, leading a life of Riley that I had never dreamed about. And . . .

"And I discovered that Louise was crying.

"I remember how astonished I was. I'd been thinking that she was as happy as I was. It was even more astonishing when she explained. 'I don't mind being married to a second-rater,' she said, 'but I can't stand being married to a PROUD one!'

"My amazed defense led to words that kept getting sharper on both sides, until we both stopped speaking. When we got home from the ride, Louise, still silent, went straight to bed. After supper, Kingsley followed her, a puzzled little girl. Sitting by the fatwood fire, I continued the debate. Booth Tarkington had told me how he'd done this with his family quarrels. I made up speeches on both sides, getting more and more acid cleverness into Louise's remarks—I always played fair in these disputes—until I suddenly remembered that tomorrow was Louise's birthday."

He had no present for her, and in the village there wasn't a shop with anything she would want. He couldn't think of any "gesture of contrition and amendment"—but one.

"I took those abandoned beginnings of ambitious stories out of the file. I found one that seemed a little less impossible than the others. During the rest of that night I gritted my teeth, and finished it. It was time for breakfast when I typed the last sentence. Louise's door was still shut, but I slid the manuscript under it.

"Louise mailed the manuscript that morning to the *Saturday Evening Post*. We knew the *Post* guaranteed a decision within forty-eight hours, and a check—to the triumphant—in a week. We held our breath long after the time a rejection would have needed. Then, in our box at the post office one day, there it was! Not a fat envelope returning the manuscript. It was too thin to hold anything but a letter."

Kahler hurried home where he would let Louise open it. It was from one of the *Post* editors, Churchill Williams. The Post would publish the story, titled *KWYW*, and would pay him $500 for it.

"It was a day to remember. Louise and I both remembered it well."

It was also the beginning of a phenomenal record worthy of The Guinness Book of Records if that book had been published in the 1930s. For Kahler followed *KWYW* (short for "Know What You Want") with 98 consecutive stories for the Post—not one rejection slip for any of the 98.

Eventually, between 1916 and 1940, he would write some 130 for the *Post*. And that wasn't all: 100-plus for *Collier's*, some 60 for the *Ladies Home Journal* and scores of others, plus four novels and a dozen novelettes.

And what ever happened to the 99th story he sent to the *Post?* Well, it came back with a letter of rejection from the editor, George Horace Lorimer. It was a surprise to Kahler and a disappointment for the friends he had made among the *Post* staffers. After number 98 had been accepted, he promised them that it if he sold the next two stories he would use the check for Number 100 "to throw a party that will rock Philadelphia to its foundations."

When Number 99 was rejected, his friends went to Lorimer and told him about the party he was spoiling. Usually Lorimer's rejections were final. "If you can't write it right the first time," the editor had often said, "there's no point in trying it again." In this case, however, he said he'd give it a second chance.

But no, number 99 failed again. "Sorry," Lorimer said, "not even for the party."

Hugh McNair Kahler was born in Germantown, Pennsylvania, in 1883 and grew up in Buffalo. He was a member of Princeton University's Class of 1904, a contemporary and friend of Booth Tarkington, later a popular novelist known for such best sellers as *The Magnificent Ambersons* and *Penrod*.

As an undergraduate, Kahler learned some things about writing that were of help in later years. He liked to recall an assignment that he and his classmates were given one day: to write an essay using a technique that they had never used before.

Kahler did so, but he was sure it would be easily spotted. When he read it to the class, everyone said it was the best thing he'd ever written but what was unusual about it?

He read it again and still no one noticed what he'd done.

Finally, he explained: He'd completed the essay and then he'd gone over it and eliminated every adverb and every adjective. In order to make this work, he said, he had to strengthen many of his verbs and nouns—a tough job but it worked.

And it worked throughout the rest of his life.

Peter Benchley, 'Jaws'
The Sunday Times Advertiser, June 3, 1973

Peter Benchley was in the kitchen of his Pennington home, pouring a second cup of breakfast coffee, when the phone rang. It was Tom Congdon, a senior editor at Doubleday, calling from Texas.

Congdon, as it turned out, was calling about Peter's novel, which Doubleday will publish next January in a clothbound edition. But first Congdon wanted to know if Peter was standing or sitting.

Standing.

"Well," said Congdon, "sit down and listen to some good news."

Benchley sat down and presently received the most pleasant shock of his life.

"They held the auction yesterday," Congdon started. The auction had been for the paperback rights to Benchley's book, a routine procedure in today's publishing world.

"Yes?"

". . . and," Congdon went on, "Bantam made the high bid of . . ."

"Yes?"

"Five hundred and seventy-five thousand dollars!"

And this, as things turned out, was to be only part of the financial story of "Jaws," a 310 page novel that hasn't even been printed yet.

For television rights there were offers ranging from $30,000 to $75,000. But these were put aside with the arrival of word that Universal and two other Hollywood companies would go to $150,000 for the movie rights. What about the screenplay? Benchley wanted to write it himself. Okay, said Universal, $25,000 plus a percentage of the picture for the screenplay. It was a deal!

Each day of late brings further good news. The Book-of-the-Month Club announces that "Jaws" will be part of a forthcoming dual selection. That means a guarantee of $42,500. The Reader's Digest Book Club takes the book for another hefty sum, and so does the Playboy Book Club.

In coming years, Benchley will split, 50-50 with his publisher, Doubleday, on the paperback, $575,000, and the money for the other subsidiary rights. But the movie money is all his, minus agent fees.

As accurately as Benchley can figure things out at this stage, and there are additional offers possible, he'll get $50,000 a year from Doubleday for seven or eight years, and who knows? Perhaps for the rest of his life if the book has a big hardcover sale, which seems likely, and if that phone keeps ringing. The best estimate of his share in the book's profits, as things now stand, is $550,000. Not bad, as some are saying, for sitting down at a typewriter and putting one little word after another.

The nearest thing to a pre-publication celebration was a luncheon date Peter had the other day at 21 in Manhattan with his father, novelist Nathaniel Benchley, and his mother.

"I thought," Peter recalls, "the least I could do, and for the first time in my life, was to pick up the check—it was for something like 87 dollars—instead of letting my father pay. But my father said no, not until that big check clears the bank. "You never know about these things," he says. So, once more he paid the check.

"And, speaking of my father, it's not surprising that he's wary of contracts, and offers, and deals and such. He has had all kinds of deals fall through, all kinds off unbelievable bad luck. He's had a novel come out right in the middle of a newspaper strike. One time his new book was shipped to bookstores in boxes mislabeled and so they were returned unopened.

"But even so, he's had something I haven't had: critical acclaim."

Nathaniel Benchley has, indeed, in the past 20 years built a solid reputation as a novelist dealing with contemporary times and themes. In achieving success as a writer, he has emulated his father, the late beloved humorist Robert Benchley who achieved fame as critic, essayist, bon vivant, and as the central character in some of the funniest movie "shorts" ever to come out of Hollywood.

At the time of Robert Benchley's death in 1945, son Nathaniel was just beginning to make it as a writer. And grandson Peter—whose first novel now promises to make more than any of Robert Benchley's works ever made—was five years old.

So, as many people are asking Peter Benchley these days, what's the story? What's it all about, this gold-plated book?

"It's an adventure story," Benchley says. "A resort on Long Island is beset by a killer shark that appears suddenly, chases the tourists off, and won't go away. It's a 122 foot shark that weighs 6,000 pounds.

"The last third of the book is the hunt for the shark conducted by a saturnine young professional fisherman, a young ichthyologist from Wood's Hole and the police chief of Amity, Long Island."

How did you come to write it?

"Well, I've been a shark freak all my adult life. I grew up in Nantucket, got to know something about the sea. And one day I got to thinking: What if . . . What if a seaside town was threatened by a huge shark? What would happen to the town, to its people, if they couldn't get rid of it? How would they react, and so forth?

"I sat on What If for six, almost seven years. I'd go to lunch with publishers, and I'd talk and they'd encourage me, nice friendly people doing their job of coaxing novels out of writers, but nothing but talk out of me. Then one day I said to myself, "This is ridiculous; you can't be a novelist without creating a novel." So I started working on what turned out to be 'Jaws.'"

Dawes' Debut, 50 Years in the Making,
The Trenton Evening Times, December 12, 1974

In the George Plimpton set on the East Side of Manhattan, so the story goes, they used to identify Jacqueline Kennedy in what might seem to be an odd way: "The one who just came in? Oh, that's Lee's sister" (and Lee, of course, was Lee Radziwill).

In a somewhat similar situation, Congressman Frank Thompson Jr. may, any day now, find himself on the wrong end of such a ploy: "The silver-haired guy who just came in? Oh that's Dawes's brother."

Yeah. Big, old Dawes Thompson—Thompy's kid brother, Rosemary Quinn's husband—has made it into the big time. As a musician. After all these years.

Old Dawes, the one with all those kids. The one with all those jazz records and tapes in his cellar up on Hillcrest Avenue, has arrived. All those hours he's devoted to jazz, all those "skiffle" sessions in the cellar, are about to pay off.

For at 8 o'clock Saturday night, when that big curtain goes up at Alice Tully Hall in Lincoln Center, there on the spotlighted stage will be Dawes, a confident smile on his face and his big old Gretsch unamplified guitar in hand, one of the seven members of Bob Greene's "World of Jelly Roll Morton" band.

A full house is anticipated because the band's last appearance at Tully Hall, last February, evoked joyous applause and comments such as this one from John S. Wilson, jazz critic of the *New York Times*: "It was a thoughtfully prepared concert, brilliantly executed and lovingly received by a house filled with seemingly knowledgeable listeners."

Dawes Thompson is best known here as a former *Newark News* reporter—a good one—and, for the past dozen years, the public relations officer of the Delaware River Basin Commission, and as a fervid and eloquent hater of anything that smacks or smells of a place called Princeton, New Jersey. ("You should have seen her, this old dame from Princeton on the jury with me. 'Do you know,' she says, 'I never before realized that Trenton is actually in Mercer County!' ")

To some people, Dawes is a genial piano player, the kind who can be persuaded to play for boozed-up party people in the mood for "The Darktown Strutters' Ball." But the piano, as much as he likes to noodle around on it, is not his forte. "Piano?" he says. "I'm just a whorehouse-blues piano player."

But with a jazz guitar, Dawes is something else; for years now he's been moonlighting as a jazz rhythm guitarist, mostly with some better-than average bands in North Jersey. He does some soloing on such gigs, but his main role "is, one, to provide the harmonic foundation and, two, some steam for the other players."

The band, which faithfully reproduces the sounds of the late Mr. Jelly Roll and his Red Hot Peppers, has been acclaimed by critics. "Brilliant re-creations of Jelly's style," says the New York Times. "If one closed one's eyes," says the man from *New Yorker* magazine, "it was Morton himself onstage." And the critic from *Storyville* magazine reports that "one can sit back and marvel at such music and such playing. The old man, if he had been alive, would have loved every moment of this concert." Aficionados of New Orleans jazz go even further in their praise.

It's fairly heady stuff, and quite frankly, Dawes Thompson is enjoying the hell out of it. Even when friends needle him a bit about being a late bloomer, about finally, after all these years, after all those children, making it. "What a nice thing," they say, some of them, only half kidding, "to happen at your age."

Nice as some of the compliments are, and pleasant as it is to be part of such an accomplished group, Dawes, at the ripe old age of 50, is finding the preparation for Saturday night's concert a lot of hard work. "It's classic New Orleans jazz," he explains, "and it's very intricate stuff to play—change of keys, and breaks and accents and slurs and so forth. We've been working day and night for weeks."

Almost every night recently, and on every weekend, Dawes has been practicing with the group in a Manhattan landmark called Nola Hall. With such a schedule in addition to his regular job at the Basin Commission headquarters he's not getting much sleep these nights, but it's all such fun he's thriving on it.

As who wouldn't in such company?

Take Bob Greene, the pianist and leader of the band. "Here," says Dawes, "is a well-known jazz pianist, a strange animal whose single purpose is to emulate the style of a great player:" Ferdinand (Jelly Roll) Morton—born 1885, died 1941. "Morton was a phenomenal pianist, sort of bridging the world of jazz and the world of ragtime and into orchestral jazz. He had a remarkably creative mind—composer of such standards as 'King Porter Stomp'—and in addition he put together, back in the 1920s, the Red Hot Peppers, generally accepted as one of the phenomena—the epitome of New Orleans jazz band creation.

"Jelly Roll was one of the best performers in jazz, not of the Louis Armstrong dimension—no one was—but he put together just the most thrilling New Orleans jazz band ever to play in a recording studio. Like Armstrong's Hot Five, Jelly Roll and his Peppers never played in public—strictly a recording band. They made a couple dozen records, and they're considered immortal.

"Over the years, Bob Greene has been appearing at jazz festivals and concerts as an unashamed Jelly Roll devotee, a pianist known for his Jelly Roll recreations.

"Well, one day George Wein, a jazz entrepreneur and a sometime pianist, suggested that Bob Greene broaden out and put together a Red Hot Peppers band. Greene went ahead and did it, and the band appeared at the Newport Jazz Festival in New York in July '73 and it was well received. Last February, in Tully Hall, at Lincoln Center, the band gave another full-scale concert and, as *Village Voice* reported, 'the audience gave Greene and his group a standing ovation.'"

And now the recreated Jelly Roll band is set for another big night at Lincoln Center, and this time with Dawes on guitar—a Walter Mitty kind of dream come true. (Not that old Dawes is all that timid; not on your flippin' life, as he might put it.)

Yeah, he told a visitor in his jazz-cluttered cellar the other day, he'd joined the band, at Greene's invitation, a month or so ago. He'd known Greene for years, seen him at jazz festivals and concerts and so forth, and sometimes they'd play together in sessions at such places as right on the Mississippi levee.

Dawes first went to the festivals and such as a listener. Then he got to playing, and pretty soon he was rhythm guitarist for such groups as the St. Louis Mudcats. And now it's the big time with the recreated Morton band.

"There are seven of us. Tommy Benford on drums. He's great. Played with Jelly Roll in the 1920s. Milt Hinton on bass. One of the best bass players in jazz. On clarinet, another New Orleans great, Herb Hall, brother of Edmund Hall, the famous New Orleans clarinetist. On trombone, Ephraim Resnick, a New York studio and pit man; in the pit band for *Hello, Dolly*—in a lot of pit bands. Good man. On piano, Bob Greene, and, on cornet, the only other part-timer besides me, a Wall Street broker named John Bucher. And that's it.

"Essentially it's a concert band. We'll be recording next week—an LP of 'Black Bottom Stomp,' 'The Original Jelly

Roll Blues,' and such. Two tours are being arranged, the first one next fall. Same tour stops as the Preservation Hall Band of New Orleans."

Thompson's interest in jazz goes back four decades, when at the age of about ten he started collecting records. "Thompy," as Dawes calls his 56-year old brother, the congressman, was a Duke Ellington fan. "When Thompy was out of the house," Dawes recalls, "I'd sneak into his room and play the records. Pretty soon I became even more fanatical than he was. By the time I was 15, I had a pretty big collection of records.

"I was a self-taught piano player and later a self-taught guitarist. And what they say about the lawyer who represents himself goes for me, too; a self-taught musician has a fool for a pupil. It's probably just as well, though. If I'd had lessons, my whole life would have been different."

Dawes lets the words trail off, but one gets the idea that he's more than content with the way things have turned out. All those great kids of his growing up in an atmosphere not unlike that of the play *You Can't Take It With You*. A big rambling house, first on Riverside Drive, more recently one at 82 Hillcrest in Trenton, full of jazz and happy sounds, and weekend guests, and month-long or longer guests. The player piano in the cellar, and all those records and tapes and other bits of happy clutter.

Jam sessions far into the night and long into the weekend. John Ellis on bass. Tony Ludwig on clarinet, Al Fish on cornet. All from around here. And sometimes Joe Scannella—Joe (Sax) Scannella, that is, not Joe (Trumpet) Scannella, his first cousin. "Joe Trumpet is a good friend, but he hasn't played in any of our sessions. Joe Sax's uncle has, though: Patsy Scannella, good bassist."

Once in a while there's a professional in from New York for a session at Dawes's place: "Dill Jones, for one. He's a Welsh pianist, a fixture in the New York scene for 15 years. Jimmy Ryan's and places like that."

And then there are the "skiffle" sessions. Sometimes at Dawes's place, sometimes at John Kolesar's in Crosswicks. "In a skiffle band," Dawes explains, "you have a casual type of jazz out of the south side of Chicago with a detour through the South. In skiffle you have legitimate jazz instruments and illegitimate instruments such as the kazoo or comb, the washboard, and other makeshift percussion instruments, a suitcase even. Much of the most beautiful jazz has been played with such instruments."

Among those in the skiffle sessions are sometime-host Kolesar, a pretty good trumpet man, Earl Josephson (son of Barney) on the comb; his brother Art Josephson on the jug, and maybe Dawes on banjo—"an instrument I usually play only at gunpoint or for money"—if the guitar isn't right at hand.

Dawes discovered the guitar while he was on duty at an Air Force base in Alaska during World War II. "Steve Randarzo, one of the guys in the barracks, was a pretty good player and got me interested, taught me a little. My mother later sent me an inexpensive guitar and pretty soon I was playing in a band. We were in the Yukon Territory and we'd get flown around, playing little dances here and there, any place where there were some WAC's. It was fun.

"After the war, a group of friends who knew about my interest in the instrument gave me a beautiful Martin guitar. That was Christmas nearly 25 years ago. Now I'm playing a really good one, a Gretsch, about 35 years old. Got it from Bill Revesz, a fine guitarist from Trenton."

In order to support his jazz habit as well as the wife and kids, Thompson decided after getting out of the service to try to get a job on a newspaper. It was a tough time to get such a job, with so many regular staffers returning from the war. And Dawes didn't have the sort of credentials that cause a prospective employer to flip. He'd attended, and got himself kicked out of, Trenton High, Trenton Catholic Boys' High and several other schools he'd rather not mention. He hadn't gone to college at all.

He had, however, grown up in a newspaper family. His father, the late Frank Thompson, was one of the ablest journalists in local history. His uncle, the late Francis A. Jamieson, won a Pulitzer Prize for his coverage of the Lindbergh kidnapping case.

And so, in 1945, Dawes tried the *Trenton Times Newspapers* and a dozen or more others. Nobody seemed to be hiring. Then, somehow, there was an offer from the *Newark News*—"a great paper," as he said the other day, "whose demise I lament."

He worked for the *News* for 16 years, the last seven at the State House, where he was the paper's bureau chief.

By 1962, Dawes and wife Rosemary had six children and expenses that were beginning to exceed your typical journalist's salary. And so Dawes did what a lot of journalists do: he took a PR job. He's been public relations officer with the Basin Commission ever since.

He's also been, since the early 1950s, "Thompy's brother." But perhaps all that will change now.

John McPhee, 'Levels of the Game'
The Trenton Times Sunday Advertiser, February 9, 1975

A sizzling day in July—95 degrees in the shade, 99 percent humidity. At his home in the woods off Drakes Corner Road, in Princeton Township, author John Angus McPhee talks about *Levels of the Game.* On publication, Donald Jackson of *Life* magazine would call it "probably the best tennis book ever written; superb." Robert Lipsyte of *The New York Times* would say of it: "this may be the high point of American sports journalism."

On the surface, *Levels* is an account of a semifinal match in the U. S. Singles Championship of 1968, an exciting match that Arthur Ashe won. But there was a lot more than tennis to the story, and getting the under-the-surface material was a job of many months, as it is with every subject McPhee writes about—from our endangered environment to the growing availability of fissionable nuclear material.

He'd been thinking of writing about two persons at the same time. He didn't care what they were: architect and client; it didn't matter. And then, after witnessing a tennis match at Forest Hills between Arthur Ashe and Clark Graebner, he decided to try it with these two contestants. Maybe they'd mirror each other.

So he got the kinescope of the match from CBS-TV. He used the film of the match as his principal research tool, and he permitted himself a certain amount of license. "I showed the film to both Ashe and Graebner several times, separately and together, and I took down their comments as those that went through their heads while playing. I decided, on the basis of what I was hearing, it was so similar to what would happen in a match that I'd take this license of having it happen in actual play. And nobody's ever complained about this, least of all Ashe and Graebner, because it has the ring of truth to it."

Finally finishing with the film, he began another part of the research. He went to Washington to talk to Arthur Ashe's aunt. He went to Gum Springs, Virginia, and stayed with Arthur's family. He slept in Arthur's bed. He rode around much of time in Arthur's father's pickup truck, asking questions, prodding a bit, jotting down notes.

After he'd soaked up as much as he felt he needed at Gum Springs, he went to interview Dr. Robert Walter Johnson, the man who trained the young Arthur Ashe on the court.

Then, on to Cleveland where McPhee talked to Clark Graebner's parents and to others who knew him.

Back home in Princeton, McPhee typed up all of his notes and got ready to start writing. And so he goes on to put together, in *Levels of the Game*, the story of two young men—one black, the other white; one the descendant of slaves, the other the son of an affluent dentist—engaged in a kind of conflict. The milieu happens to be tennis, but basically what he's writing about is a confrontation between two human beings and about their backgrounds and their natures.

And, led on by McPhee's word magic, the reader sees the first ball of the match lifted into the air and struck with a racquet, and seems to be following an exciting tennis match. But there's more to it than that. Transported by McPhee's narrative, not to mention the solid research behind it, the reader finds himself, between points at Forest Hills, back at the slave ship that brought Arthur Ashe's great-great-great grandmother here from Africa.

The story flows. There are flashbacks to earlier days, to country club scenes, to snubs and disappointments, to happy moments. There are flash-forwards and other techniques used in telling this many-leveled story, but it's all done with such grace, such style and imagination that there are no lapses, no sudden jerks; it all goes together; the transitions are smooth; the hard work that has gone into it makes it all mesh and seem effortless.

And all these things can be said of just about anything John McPhee writes, from his first book (about a basketball player named Bill Bradley) to his latest, *The Curve of Binding Energy*, a brilliantly recorded journey into the awesome and alarming world of a nuclear scientist named Theodore B. Taylor.

Each of his books leads the reader into an unlikely world (the Pine Barrens) or on to an unlikely subject (a whole book about oranges, for example,) but invariably the reader is glad to have made the trip.

Notes for a Future Historian,
Sunday Times Advertiser, April 25, 1976

(Bill took a stroll through the city of Trenton noting changes along the way.)

It is Easter Monday, April 19, 1976. Hot. Hottest April 19 in recorded history: 88 degrees and rising.

On Perry Street it seems even hotter. There is the angry and repeated sound of automobile horns. The air is saturated with the odor of hot olive oil. It is coming from the Freeway Steak House, across from the entrance to the Trenton Freeway. The Steak House, featuring Puerto Rican dishes, was, in bygone days, the home of a German family, the Metzlers.

Lines of autos, eastbound and westbound, await the changing of the traffic light at Perry and Stockton. In one of the halted cars, an elderly black man and his wife sit impassively and apparently unaware that a jet of hot steam is hissing out of the radiator of their tired old car.

The lines of traffic fail to move even when the light turns green. The horns sound off again. There are shouts and curses. Seated in a car behind the black couple, a white man leans hard on his horn, steps out of his car and shouts: "Get that bleeping truck off the bleeping street!" It is his way of calling attention to a Bond Bread truck that is double-parked and clogging traffic. His plea supported by another blare of snarling horns. But nothing moves.

Groups of blacks look on from front-door steps and street corners. An old man seated in front of one house swigs a bottle of wine in a brown paper bag. Further along on Perry, past Stockton, three Puerto Rican girls, looking fresh and beautiful even in this heat, are jumping rope.

Perry Street. This is where my father grew up. How many times did he walk along here, on the way from his home in

Goosetown (further east on Perry) to St. Mary's Cathedral Grammar School? This area was largely Irish and German then, and right up to World War II the neighborhood remained largely white.

Now it is black and Puerto Rican. Speckle Red's soul food restaurant was Carrie Gilbert's delicatessen back in the 1930s. The Puerto Rican Church (Iglesia de Nuestra Senora del Monte Carmelo) was the Heitzman Brothers' furniture store. What once was the shop of Howard's Cycle Company is now the San Juan Café. Trenton Vacuum Cleaners is now the site of Los Isabelinos Restaurant and Social Club.

As a non-black, non-Puerto Rican, I am out of place in my father's onetime neighborhood. I am reminded of this when I go into a shoemaker's shop to get a shine. The proprietor, a black man in his sixties, is shining the shoes of an older black man, seated in one of the shop's two chairs.

Pointing to the empty chair, I ask, "Got room for one more?"

"No," says the shoemaker, pausing at his task. "It's too hot. After I get finished with this gentleman, I have to get back to those." He points to a pair of partially repaired shoes.

"You can't give me a shine?"

"No, it's too hot."

As I leave the place, I hear him mutter. "Every once in a while I get one."

I continue west along Perry. There is a crowd of well-dressed people in front of the African Methodist Episcopal Church. A few buildings closer to Broad Street, all is quiet in front of another black church. Friendship Baptist. In the front window of its annex there is a sign that reads: "The church where everybody is somebody."

I pass the old bus terminal where I used to get the bus for Trenton State Teachers College in Hillwood Lakes. No buses now. Lots of taxicabs.

Is Stanley the numbers writer still in business here? No sign of him. Used to be here all the time, his pockets stuffed with 3-by-5 scratch pads. Where are you, Stanley? Doesn't anything remain the same?

The old Hanover Trust building stands at the northeast corner of Perry and Broad, but the bank is long gone. My father and a lot of his friends lost money when it went under.

Its windows are covered with sheets of corrugated metal. A dead neon sign reading ARMY SUPPLIES remains from the building's days as a shoddy general store. A sign at the front door reads "North Trenton Neighborhood Family Health Center," but the place is locked tight.

"The health center still in there?" I ask an old black man standing near the corner.

"No," he says, "it's closed. Everything's closed. And you know why?"

"Why?"

"Because they ain't got no law. That's why."

"You mean they don't enforce the law?"

"They don't enforce the law, they don't have no law."

North Broad Street and Perry. Two cars race through a red light, one of them forcing two pedestrians back on the sidewalk. One pedestrian shouts an obscenity, but the red-light-jumpers are barreling toward the Battle Monument.

The Battle Monument. It's just about where Colonel Henry Knox's cannons were set up on the morning of Thursday, December 26, 1776. American artillerymen fired ball and grapeshot down Broad Street (Queen Street in those days) and Warren Street (King Street). The Hessians, taken by surprise, were never able to set up a defense. In about an hour the whole thing was over; the first Battle of Trenton, it would be called.

Perry and Warren. On the southeast corner here stood a tavern in the mid-1700s. Just before the Revolution it was the home of Pontius Delare Stille, Trenton's first treasurer. At the time of Washington's surprise attack, it was the headquarters guardhouse of the Hessians who occupied the town. No building stands there now; it is part of the St. Michael's Churchyard.

Across the street there was the Stacy Potts House, the headquarters of Colonel Rall, commanding officer of the three Hessian regiments billeted in Trenton. In front of this house a captain named William Washington (distant cousin of George Washington) and an 18-year old lieutenant named James Monroe (later the fifth President of the United States) were wounded while putting two Hessian cannons out of business.

Not far from where this happened, two dudes in high heels are swigging cans of Shasta and taking in the scene. Do they know what went on here during that stormy morning of December 26, 1776? Do any of these people driving through?

Walking down Warren toward Hanover, I am reminded of the Sunday afternoon years ago when I and my classmates, in black caps and gowns, marched along here (to the tune of "The Bells of St. Mary's") from St. Mary's Cathedral High School to the Lincoln Theater to receive our diplomas. Governor A. Harry Moore was the speaker that day, and he made us all bawl when he told of his life as a poor boy growing up in a North Jersey slum. And now here he was, the Governor of the State of New Jersey. He cried. We all cried. He was One of Us (translation: Irish Catholic), and he could really lay it on.

Warren and Hanover. On the southeast corner stands the Taylor Pork Roll Sandwich Shop. Above the shop are floors, mainly inhabited these days by pigeons.

This was once the Trenton House, one of the city's finest hotels. On February 21, 1861, president-elect Abraham Lincoln dined here, and afterward, from a balcony, spoke informally to a large and generally admiring audience. The crowd was pressed close together and pickpockets had a big day.

Shortly before coming to the Trenton House, Lincoln had addressed the Legislators at the State House.

"I cannot but remember the place New Jersey holds in the early history of our country," he said to the legislators. "I remember that in the Revolutionary struggle none had more of its battlefields. I remember reading, in my youth, a small book—*The Life of Washington*—and of his struggles none fixed itself on my mind so indelibly as the crossing of the Delaware preceding the Battle of Trenton. I remember that these great struggles were made for some object. I am exceedingly anxious that the object they fought for—liberty, and the Union and Constitution they formed—shall be perpetual."

Standing before the former Trenton House now, a smartly dressed black girl of about 20 is pretending she doesn't hear what the two black men in the Cadillac with four, big fat white-walled tires are saying: "C'mon, honey, you wanta take a ride?" "C'mon, honey, come with us."

She ignores them and they move on when horns behind them begin to sound. Crisis over. She shakes her head and crosses the street toward what was once the Lincoln Theater.

Bing Crosby was one of the Rhythm Boys when Paul Whiteman and his men played there. Spencer Tracy was a member of the resident company at the Trent Theater, further down Warren, a short time before he went to Hollywood.

Continuing on the east side of Warren Street, I pass Stuckert's fabulous drug store where the skinny guy used to make the best bacon, lettuce and tomato in town. Now the place is Wig City Boutique.

Next, the Comfort Station. But it's all boarded up. I recall the time years ago, when one of the Sisters of Mercy at Cathedral High warned us never to go near the place. Why? we asked. Because all sorts of men steal down the alley and go into the place. She had no idea that it was nothing more than a men's rest room.

It's gone now. So is the comfort station (for women as well as men) that used to stand in the middle of Montgomery Street, in the shadow of the Broad Street Bank Building. Where, one wonders, do people go these days?

On to the Trenton Commons and memories of places that used to be there. Child's Restaurant, the place where you went after New Year's Eve parties and high school proms. Across the street, Bear-Mey's Tea Room, where you went for a milkshake and sandwich after high school dances and basketball games. Its greatest attraction was a beautiful waitress named Betty. Where is she today?

Going down "the hill" of South Warren Street toward Front, one passes the site of Trenton's first public building: The Hunterdon County Court House. A sort of Borough Hall cum-slammer. (Trenton was the county seat of Hunterdon before Mercer County was formed in the late 1830s.)

It was (as historian John O. Raum noted) "a two story building erected of grey sandstone with stuccoed front. The cells were in the lower story. The upper story was used as a courtroom, the entrance to which was, by a number of stone steps erected on the outside of the building and surmounted by an iron railing."

This was the site of occasional executions in the 1770s, one of which attracted not only the usual large crowd but also the celebrated Methodist preacher, George Whitefield. That was on Nov. 21, 1739, and here is what Whitefield noted in his diary for that day:

> Being strongly desired by many, and hearing that a condemned malefactor was to suffer that week, I went in company with about 30 to Trenton, and reached thither by five in the evening.
>
> Here God pleased to humble my soul, and bring my sins to remembrance, so that I could hardly hold up my head. However, knowing that God called, I went out, trusting in Divine strength, and preached in the courthouse [sic]; and though I was quite barren and dry in the beginning of the discourse, yet God enabled me to speak with great sweetness, freedom and power before I had done.
>
> The unhappy criminal seemed hardened, but I hope some good was done in the place.

On this same site, years later—on July 8, 1776—the Declaration of Independence was read for the first time outside Philadelphia.

And what is there on this historic site today? A parking lot. Parts of the wall of the old courthouse are still visible at the rear of the lot.

The parking lot entrance on Warren Street is bounded by two places that bring back memories. One, now known as the Brass Rail, used to be Sharkey Kelly's bar. Sharkey was a retired policeman, a celebrated man in the town. He was said to have been a good cop, but there were endless stories of how he had treated some of those he arrested. "Boy," any number of insiders would tell you, "how old Sharkey could beat those niggers up!" Such stories were told admiringly, and they brought no honor to Sharkey or to those who told them.

On the other side of what was once the courthouse site, 26 South Warren, stood one of Trenton's biggest bookie joints and gambling centers. Everybody in town, including the cops, knew what was going on there, but the place flourished for years.

On the way to the destination of this serendipitous stroll, Mill Hill Park, I pass some other places that bring certain pictures to mind:

Stout and Company, tailors, Front and Warren: On this site for many years the *Trenton Daily True American* was published. This was a Democratic paper that was sometimes vehemently opposed to President Lincoln and in favor of the South during the Civil War. One night after a particularly vicious editorial appeared, a mob surrounded the place, smashed up the building, and threatened to burn it down.

Gus Alberti's restaurant on Front Street: Here, for about a dollar, you could get a complete dinner. Later, in the 1940s, the place was converted into a bar that was mobbed on nights when such a star as Ella Fitzgerald performed.

Continuing the stroll, I witness some unpleasantness on the roadway and a near accident. A driver deliberately pulls from the curb into a line of traffic, almost giving an oncoming driver a case of apoplexy. Two young drivers suffering from speed conceit "make rubber" as the light changes, almost knocking down pedestrians as they race down Warren Street. There are shouts and curses.

A truck suddenly darts into the path of a taxi. Brakes screech. Horns blow. The drivers curse each other.

And then, Mill Hill Park: It is green, acres and acres of rolling green, right in the heart of the city. It is quiet. An oasis.

The park borders the Assunpink Creek, from Stockton Street almost to the Delaware River. There is a playground where kids are chasing themselves around corners and riding down sliding boards. There is an amphitheater built into the west bank of the creek a short distance from the Broad Street bridge. Three men—bongo drums, gourd, and spoon—are playing Spanish songs in the front of the amphitheater. All alone. Playing just for themselves and a few passersby who stop to listen.

There are meandering paths where kids on bicycles are riding and others are strolling. There are benches for those who just want to sit and look.

And, out on the grassy field, there are these kids, black and white, dancing and playing together. As I walk across the field, some of them come running up.

"Hey, mister, can you tell us something?"

"What?"

"Can you tell us what that stone's for?"

The stone is a pinkish-grey piece of marble with a smooth top.

A girl explains: "They put that in last week and there's nothing on it. What's it for?"

Well, I say, it's probably going to tell something about what happened here. Did they know anything about what happened around here about 200 years ago?

"I know," one girl says. "George Washington discovered America, right?"

"No," another says, "Columbus did that."

Did anybody know what happened right here in Mill Hill Park?

"I know: Betsy Ross made the first flag here."

"No, Betsy Ross freed the slaves, didn't she?"

"Betsy Ross freed the slaves? She didn't free no slaves. That was Harriett Thompson."

"Harriet Taubman [sic], you mean?"

"Yeah, Harriett Taubman."

So it goes until it is explained that the second battle of Trenton was fought, most of it, right around here: "You see that hill on the other side of the creek? That's where George Washington and his troops were in the afternoon and evening of January the second, 1777. And Cornwallis and the British and Hessians were on this side.

"See that bridge on Broad Street? The British tried to storm it and wipe out Washington's army but they couldn't cross the bridge. The American fire held them off.

"And when it got dark, Washington left his campfires burning and moved quietly with his army down that way and the next morning surprised the British at Princeton."

"You mean that all happened right here?"

"Yes, it did. And this is where your teachers ought to bring you and tell you all."

Ann Packard, Portrait of the Artist as Woman,
The Trentonian, March 3, 1977

(Bill's piece concentrating on the loss of her son appeared in the *New York Times,* March 13, 1977.)

A five-alarm fire in Princeton, the worst in 30 years, at least six buildings on Witherspoon and Spring Sts. gutted and falling apart.

"Oh, my God!" Anne Locke Packard said when her friend Peggy Hansen called around eight in the morning to tell her about it. "What about the gallery?"

"No word yet on the radio about the gallery," Peggy said. "But there's to be another report in a few minutes."

In the kitchen of her home in Hopewell, Anne Packard went on with the job of getting breakfast ready for the kids. No, she wouldn't turn on the radio. "If I don't know it," she told herself, "then it hasn't happened."

But, she learned later in the morning, after driving to Princeton with Peggy, it had happened. As they approached the fire scene, she stopped, closed her eyes and asked, "Is it there?"

"No, Anne," Peggy said, "it's gone."

The Princeton Gallery of Fine Art, along with a dozen other businesses, was gone—a mass of twisted metal and charred bricks. A total loss.

"Oh my God!—all those paintings!"

The paintings were the work—the best work—of Max Bohm, Anne Packard's grandfather, an internationally recognized romantic impressionist whose work had hung in the Metropolitan and other leading museums of art.

She was proud of his work and wanted the art world to be reminded of his genius. A year earlier, she had taken some 20 of his paintings from the family collection and had them exhibited at the Squibb Gallery in Lawrence. It had been a successful show.

Early this year she arranged an exhibition of Bohm's paintings—14 of his best, worth, she estimated, about $100,000—at the Princeton Gallery of Fine Art on Spring St.

And now, in the morning of January 4, 1977, the gallery was gone and so were all the paintings. The family nest egg was gone. The paintings had not been insured, either by the gallery or by the family.

"Oh, my God. Let's go have a drink," was all Anne Packard could say.

Would she sue the gallery?

No, she would not: "We have to be kind to one another."

Back home in her kitchen-studio a few hours later, she picked up a long brush and went on with the seascape she was painting. No time to lose; she had a deadline for another show.

That show, her seventh one-woman exhibition in three years, will open Sunday afternoon, 3 to 5 P.M., at Gallery 100, 100 Nassau St. in Princeton, one block from the scene of the fire. "Solitudes," the show is called, and it will include 35 of her latest paintings—seascapes, harbor scenes, dunes, landscapes—works that have evoked such adjectives as *haunting, lonely, introspective, brooding, reflective* and *nostalgic.* Most of them deal with the sea: "It means everything to me, the sea. It says everything, expresses all moods."

The loss of the Bohm paintings, great as it was, was minimal compared to some of the other things that have happened to Anne Packard in the past three years—the most troubled period of her life but one during which she has somehow, she feels, found herself both as an artist and as a person.

In March, 1974, her marriage of 20 years, tottering for some time, fell apart. Her husband moved out of the house, out of town, eventually to begin a new life in France. She, just turned 40, continued to live with the five children in the big white house on the hill at 57 W. Broad St., Hopewell's main thoroughfare.

Three months later, on a sunny Saturday morning in June, she said goodbye to the eldest of her children, Stephen, 18, and his girl, Linda Lovell. They were going to hitchhike to the coast and hike the Pacific Trail, from Mexico to Oregon.

"I can still see them standing here in the study," she told a visitor the other day. "Stevie had that big pack on his back. He was so big and tall and beautiful, six-four, dirty blond hair, brown eyes.

"They had knapsacks, sleeping bags—everything was packed and ready to go. We kissed goodbye, and they walked out and went across the street and started walking. I went out and walked along on the other side of the street, watching to see if they would get a ride. I saw them put their thumbs out, and they got a ride and that was it."

It was no big deal. She returned to her kitchen-studio and resumed painting. No reason to worry about Stephen, he could take care of himself: All-state lacrosse player, graduate of Outward Bound, going to be a forester some day, he said.

In the days that followed, Stephen and Linda made their way west and Stephen wrote home about every three days. He was in high spirits; the trip was going well. He and his mother had a close, loving relationship, and it was obvious he enjoyed telling her about his experiences.

But after about three weeks there were no more postal cards. As part of their trip the pair had planned to see Linda's family in Montana. But they didn't arrive there at the appointed time, and they have not been heard from since. Stephen's last postal card home was mailed from Westport, an isolated place on the California coast. The last traveler's check he used was cashed there, too. The other checks he was carrying—some $600 worth—have not yet been cashed.

The N.J. State Police called the Packard home as recently as last week to report—again—that American Express had reported—again—that there was no new word about the un-cashed checks.

Meanwhile, there had been another tragedy. Four days after Stephen left, the boyfriend of Cynthia, the eldest of the three Packard girls, went off to work as a carpenter and was electrocuted on the job.

A rough time, the summer of '74 and, as it turned out for Anne Packard, a busy one, too: "I had a show coming up in September and so I had a lot of work to do. I lost myself in the work, painting day and night. It was good that I had the deadline, had to get the work done. It was the reason I was able to . . . well, it saved my sanity."

The three years that ensued, she says, have been the most exciting and productive of her life. The worst part was, and still is, not being able to know for sure about Stephen and Linda, not having "a chance for real grief. But I've discovered during this time, among other things, that I can fulfill roles other than mommy and wife, and, well, that I'm a worthwhile person.

"I always wanted to paint seriously, but there never was enough time for it. It always came last. The marriage had to end before I could do my work and become a real person, an individual.

"I used to be anxious about having people accept me. I don't feel that way now. I don't have any anxiety about where I fit in. I fit into myself.

"I really enjoy being responsible for the whole family, making decisions, facing reality. I love it. I love the challenge. I haven't found a way to beat the system; it's a hell of a struggle. But worth it. I've found fulfillment in my kids and in my work. It's a great feeling."

Some signs of the struggle are visible in the lines around Anne Packard's eyes and inside her home. Opening the front door for a visitor the other day, she pulled the brass knob out of the door. "Damn! There it goes again." In the big bright kitchen-studio one learns that the dishwasher doesn't work, the oven doesn't work, nor do two of the stove's four burners.

But Anne Packard works there, and her "nest" as she calls it is cluttered in the manner of Fibber McGee's closet. The clutter includes a couple of BB rifles, empty cans and cartons, her grandmother's huge palette, an electric heater that doesn't work, a dozen or more completed canvases awaiting frames, and, on rainy days, her son Michael's Yamaha Mini Enduro motorcycle.

Michael, 13, and the three Packard sisters, ranging in age up to 19, come and go. Old friends drop in to chat. Anne Packard answers their questions and comments but goes right on painting, "lost," as she says, in her work. "It's my Yoga, my TM."

Despite the clutter and other such problems as having to stretch the food money—"We eat lots of lentil soup"—she has managed to make it as a full-time freelance artist. In the past three years of "total commitment" to art, she has won a lot of first prizes and honorable mentions, she has become one of the six members of the Artists' Guild Gallery of Princeton, and she has sold paintings, hundreds of them, ranging in size from 5 x 8 inches to huge canvases, and in price from $25 to $500.

"Sure," she says, "I'm out to make a buck—have to—but it's more than that. I'm really serious about my work, committed. I want to paint paintings, not just pictures. I'm consumed with this desire to make a statement—a statement about man's aloneness—a positive statement that you don't have to have people and things to complete you, that you can find completion in yourself. I've found it in my painting and in my kids. I'm not threatened by the outside world any more.

"And when people ask me how long did it take to do this painting or that, I just look 'em straight in the eye and say, 'All my life.'"

Anne Packard grew up in an atmosphere of art. There was, for one thing, the example of her grandfather, Max Bohm. Her mother and grandmother were artists, too, though not well known.

At age five in Provincetown, Massachusetts, she posed occasionally for Phillip Malicoat, a highly regarded painter. In recent years Malicoat, now 72—"and a wonderful teacher"—has been her mentor.

In her teens in Provincetown, where the family spent most of the summers, she began to paint some of the things she saw. Her seascapes done in acrylics on pieces of driftwood sold for $5. In later years, she switched from the driftwood—"too gimmicky"—to canvas, and she went on to recording the haunting sea-related scenes that would become her specialty.

One golden summer day something happened that made her think that she might, after all, make it as an artist some day. In front of the house she was renting, she displayed a dozen or more of her seascapes. In the afternoon a man—stooped, gray, seventyish—came along, stopped and looked carefully at her work. Presently he selected one, two, three, four of the paintings, paid for them, and carried them off. What was his name? He didn't want to say.

But a day later there he was, walking along across the street. Who was that man? Why, she learned from a friend, that was Robert Motherwell, the great abstract painter, in person.

"My God!" That was all Anne Packard could say.

The Minuet in G and Me,
The Trentonian, Oct. 13, 1977

It's been a long struggle, my attempt to learn to play the piano, but I think I've finally found the help I need and it costs only 50 cents a week.

The business between the piano and me began when I was a third-grader at the Blessed Sacrament School in Trenton. I took piano lessons under protest and instead of practicing at the keyboard of an afternoon I played tennis or baseball or whatever. Anything but piano practice.

And when 3:30 P.M. rolled around every Thursday, I found myself trying to bluff my way through a half-hour of hell. I sat there on the piano stool in company with two invincible enemies. One was the piano. The other was a nun seated at my right and holding a 15-inch ruler in her right hand.

I would sometimes play as many as eight notes without being cracked on the knuckles. Then I'd hit a sour one and, crack!, the ruler would whack my knuckles again. And again and again if I continued to hit notes that weren't on the sheet.

Somehow I managed to continue the struggle until the Saturday afternoon of the dress rehearsal of a forthcoming recital. As I waited for my turn at the piano, about tenth in line, I discovered I "had to go to the basement," as we used to say in those days. I raised my hand and said "Stir," which was the way we pronounced "Sister" in those days. Presently the nun looked my way and, squirming as only a third-grader can squirm, I asked if I could go to the basement.

The answer was NO, get back in line. It was the same when I asked again. And again.

By the time it was my turn at the piano I was on the verge of bursting. I raced to the piano stool, clamped my legs together, and proceeded to race through the only number

I had managed to learn: Minuet in G. Dah-dah-DUM-ty-DUM-ty-DUM-ty-DUM . . . I played it as if it were The Flight of the Bumblebee. And this, I soon learned, just would not do. No, no, no said the nun; much too fast.

She turned the metronome on to the right tempo, a slow click-clack, and told me to keep in time with it. I did. I made it through Minuet in G, too, but not before losing control and dousing the piano seat. With the final note, I got up, beet red with embarrassment, and ran all the way home. The only other thing I remember about the incident was that the girl in line behind me, the next one to sit on that piano stool, eventually married one of my fellow journalists (presumably having recovered from the effects of the sodden seat, but somehow I never did get around to asking about it).

That was the end of my piano lessons, or rather the end of Phase One.

Phase Two began about 20 years later, during the period between college graduation and induction into the Army for World War II. After hearing my friend Ed McCardell play one New Year's Eve at the Horseshoe Bar, I decided to try the piano again. I called up a teacher and arranged for weekly lessons.

This time I practiced between lessons and the teacher, a baldish man in his 50s, was complimentary about the progress I was making. I got to the sixth or seventh lesson, and to the Minuet in G again, when IT happened.

I was sitting there minding my sharps and flats and, I thought, doing rather well. But I could tell something was wrong. It was my breathing I learned as Baldish halted the minuet.

My breathing?

Yes, Baldish explained, breathing correctly was most important. He would show me how.

As I resumed the minuet, I found that, in addition to the notes on the music sheet, I now had something else to worry about: the teacher's hands! He placed them on my crotch "to help with the breathing," and, before I realized that this was a full-scale homosexual approach, I frantically tried to keep an eye on the notes, the keys, my fingers, and on whatever the hell he was trying to do Down There.

I did not punch him in the nose (as the father of a friend of mine once did, I later learned). I just left. So ended Phase Two.

A marvelous woman named Mrs. Marti is now the key to Phase Three. She is teaching my six-year-old daughter Suzy to play the piano. And, for 50 cents a lesson, Suzy is passing on to me what she learns from Mrs. Marti.

It's wonderful. In just a few weeks of instruction I've mastered "Off to the Circus" and "I Had a Little Grey Pony." I can tell a one-count note from a two-count note, and I can practically find middle C blindfolded.

And who knows? Some day I may be able to bang out "Minuet in G" by heart.

The Last Mile, Pray for Us,
The New York Times, Sunday, August 7, 1977

Our long wait was over. The sound of voices was coming closer, but the words were still indistinct. Then the side door was opened and we could hear them clearly. They were reciting the litany of the saints.

"Saint Michael."

"Pray for us."

"Saint Gabriel."

"Pray for us."

The old priest entered the room first. He was reading from a little black prayer book that he held with both hands.

"Saint Paul," he went on, not looking up.

The priest was followed by a giant of a young man—well over six feet and powerfully muscled—who was being led into the room by two men in dark uniforms.

"Pray for us," the young man responded.

"Saint Andrew."

"Pray for us."

We had been sitting there in the small, well-lighted room, waiting for them for almost a half-hour. I was one of six or seven newspapermen there on assignment. Most of the rest of those in the crowded room—all men, about 100 of them—were policemen. Some had come from distant places to witness what was about to happen.

All of us had received form letters that read: "You are hereby invited to witness the death by electricity of _____

_____." The name of the young man now entering the room and responding to the litany had been written into the blank space.

And now we were all seated on straight-back wooden chairs in a little room in Trenton State Prison next to what they called the "Death House." I was seated front row, center, directly facing the wooden electric chair, which was about 10 feet away. I hadn't expected to be so close to it.

The young man being led to the chair had been a member of the United States Marine Corps, and he had served in the Pacific during World War II. On VJ night—the night America celebrated the surrender of the Japanese—he had gone bar-hopping with some friends. By the time the night ended, a young waitress was found dead in an abandoned well, and the Marine faced a charge of murder in the first degree.

Convicted months later and sentenced to death, he became a convert to Roman Catholicism during the days he waited for his final night. His family made repeated appeals to Gov. Alfred E. Driscoll, but in vain. There had been talk of a last-minute reprieve from the Governor's office, but it hadn't come.

And now, a few minutes past 8, here was the big Marine coming into the room, his closely shaven head glistening bright and pink under the strong ceiling lights. He was blinking and, it seemed, blushing in embarrassment, stage-frightened.

He took one appalled look at the mass of upturned faces that filled the room and, head down, all but ran to the chair. He was like a shy, scared child.

Seated in the big chair, head down and eyes closed, the Marine looked like a young, oversized Mr. Clean. His bald head blazed with reflected light. As two prison guards proceeded to strap his legs and arms to the chair, he kept responding as the priest, standing nearby, his head buried in the prayer book, continued the litany.

"Saint Agatha."

"Pray for us."

"Saint Agnes."

"Pray for us."

"Saint Cecilia . . . ."

But this time, there was no response. One of the leather straps was placed over the Marine's mouth and tightened.

The priest continued to read: "Be merciful, spare us, Oh Lord . . . ." It didn't take long. The executioner, standing only inches to the rear of the Marine, made several vigorous turns of a metal wheel that electrified the chair. The Marine's body seemed to swell and there was the sound of stretching leather straps. The skin that was visible turned from pink to purplish red.

The executioner paused for about a minute. Then he whirled the wheel again.

There was another pause. And total silence. It was broken by a bespectacled man who stepped forward and checked the Marine's body in several places. He was the prison physician. Presently, he turned to the audience and said: "this man is dead."

The priest continued to read from the little black book, but now his lips moved in silence.

Albert Herpin, The Man who Never Slept,
The Trentonian, Sept. 10, 1980

Albert Edmelare Herpin lived into his nineties and never slept a wink in all his life. He didn't use a bed; never owned one. He sat up all night, every night, reading newspapers, and never used eyeglasses. Not only that: he never used a toothbrush, never lost a tooth, never had a toothache, and never had a day's illness.

So he claimed right up to the end, and no one ever proved otherwise. According to T. Howard Waldron, back in the 1890s, Joseph Pulitzer, publisher of the *New York Word,* sent a team of European doctors here to test Herpin's claim of sleeplessness. Waldron, the City of Trenton's Director of Public Safety and in bygone days Herpin's unofficial biographer, will tell you that those doctors "maintained a 24-hour daily watch on Herpin here for a whole week. They found he never slept a wink and abandoned their inquiry completely baffled."

Howard Waldron covered the Herpin story in depth for the late, lamented *Trenton News,* a weekly that was founded, published and edited by his father, the late Thomas F. Waldron. (The paper became one of the casualties of World War II.)

In an article published in the *News* on February 24, 1939, Waldron reported:

> The only time Mr. Herpin closes his eyes is when muscular actions cause him to blink momentarily. For 70 years he has sat up all night every night and read newspapers by the light of an oil lamp. He never retired to bed. His rest is obtained by sitting in a Morris chair.
>
> Drugs and hypodermic injections have been tried by physicians over the years to induce Herpin to sleep

but were unsuccessful . . . . Mr. Herpin smokes a pipe but never touches liquor. He eats five meals a day and is always hungry, but he restricts his diet. Usually, he partakes of crackers and tea with small amounts of fruit and meat.

Countless newspaper reporters have obtained interviews from him, he has appeared in motion picture films, and he has had his story told in the cartoon drawings of Robert Ripley and John Hix. But never has anyone ever been able to discredit Herpin's story of always being awake.

Albert Herpin had this advice for insomniacs: "If you can't sleep, just relax. Keep the mind blank. Don't become excited and don't worry because all human beings lose sleep at some time or other in their lives."

As for his own condition: "Nature never demands sleep from me. The outstanding doctors of America and Europe have examined me through the years, but not one has been able to do more than guess about my condition, and no satisfactory explanation has ever been made."

He contended that shortly before his birth his mother was injured in a collision while riding in a horse-drawn vehicle in Philadelphia. He was born prematurely and, so he said, doctors noticed even in his first few months that he appeared to be awake at all times.

Herpin's grandfather, Dr. Wendell Whiteman Fraley (a veterinarian who compounded "Fraley's Family Elixir" circa 1876), was said to be the first to notice the child's round-the-clock wide-awakeness. Fraley had the infant examined by "leading doctors" who, so the story goes, all predicted that little Albert would not live for more than a week.

Albert Herpin was born near the Lalor Tract, in South Trenton, on November 15, 1851. He claimed his mother made him promise as a youth that he would never capitalize on his unusual condition. There were numerous offers of money from fairs and expositions and freak-show entrepreneurs, but Herpin turned them all down. "Never took a cent for any of the pictures of articles," he used to say, "because of that promise to my mother. I've always kept my word although some of the offers were very attractive and many times I needed the money."

For many years Herpin worked as a china decorator in one or another of Trenton's many potteries. He specialized in stipple work. Later in life, for a period of some 20 years, he worked in the City of Trenton's street department.

In his final years, about 30 of them, Herpin worked as a handyman for well-to-do families living on and near Perdicaris Place in the western section of Trenton. He took care of the furnaces, put out the garbage and ashes, tended the lawns, and shoveled the snow for dozens of families. He was still hard at it June of 1941, a few months before his 90th birthday. This is what Howard Waldron reported at that time:

> Some idea of the rugged physique possessed by Herpin . . . can be obtained from his routine during the past few months. Forty-six years ago (in 1895), Herpin built himself a stable on May Street, behind the Essex Rubber Company plant. It is an unusual building constructed of boxes, wood, and scrap iron, and it has now become his home.
>
> The water for this modest Ewing Township dwelling was furnished by a single water pipe that became clogged up and was finally shut off last October. Since then Herpin has been carrying two gallons of water to his home daily from residences on Perdicaris Place.
>
> 'I've got to have water for my tea,' he explained when asked why he carted the water so far. He always has

a pot of tea simmering on the stove, and he carried water every day during the winter, no matter how deep the snow. Quite a feat for a chap entering his 90th year.

Albert Herpin looked forward to living a century. "There's not much for me to look forward to now as I grow older," he used to say, "but I would like to reach the one hundred year mark. Wouldn't that be something, a century without a wink of sleep?"

But Herpin wasn't to last that long. On the first day of February, 1942, he was taken from his shack under protest—he said he was feeling okay—and driven to Mercer Hospital where he spent his final days.

Other notes re: Herpin:

Doctors are fond of saying that sleep is the brain's food; starve the brain and you die. So what are we to make of the strange case of Al Herpin, a 90-year-old handyman of average intelligence and excellent health? When word spread of this ancient who claimed he had never slept, legions of doctors marched to his door, determined to expose the fraud and thus buttress their own medical theories.

Inside Herpin's house, the doctors found a rocking chair and a table—but no bed, no hammock no cot, nothing on which a man might lie down. For weeks on end, medics attended Herpin in relays, waiting for the man to sneak a few winks. He never did. Naturally, after a hard day's work at odd jobs, he would be tired. But his way of resting was to sit in his rocker and read seven newspapers thoroughly until he felt refreshed.

His was one of the most extraordinary cases in medical history. Herpin finally closed his eyes for eternal sleep on January 3, 1947, at the age of 94.

Leicester Hemingway, Memories of Les,
The Trentonian, November 17, 1982

News of the death of Les Hemingway got me to thinking about him: laughing about some of his ploys and escapades and painfully recalling some of the tragic elements of his life.

One of the memories was of a sunny day in June 1945 when Les and I and the rest of the Fourth Infantry Division's headquarters GIs were living in Bamberg, Germany, in what had been an army training center—a *"Kaserne,"* I think it was called. The war in Europe had ended about a month earlier and there wasn't much work to be done except to prepare for a scheduled move to the Pacific for the invasion of Japan.

Private Leicester Hemingway, functioning (more or less) as division photographer, was on this June day preparing to photograph Major General Howard Blakely, the division commander, surrounded by his staff officers and field officers—majors and colonels—on duty with the division's regiments: the 8th, 12th and 22nd. The officers in their best uniforms and squinting into the sun were seated with General Blakely on the spacious front steps of a headquarters building. Most of them had ridden in from battalion and regimental headquarters situated five to 20 miles away.

Private Hemingway was, as usual on these occasions, giving directions, and thoroughly enjoying himself. "Ass over to the left a bit, Colonel, will you please?" "Chin up, Major. Ah that's better."

As he waited for Les to complete his directions, General Blakely asked: "Hemingway, what the hell happens to all the photos you take?" The general had posed for numerous Hemingway specials, but, as he now said, "I never see any of them."

"Well, General," Les replied, "you know how it is in the Army. I send the film back to Paris but I never get it back."

The general looked a bit skeptical.

Les finally got the officers into position and started clicking the camera. The session lasted almost a half hour and toward the end the officers, steaming in their woolens, began to mutter.

"Okay," Les finally said, "that's it," and the officers groaned in relief.

A few minutes later, in a room we used as an office, Les opened up the camera and, with a triumphant smile, showed me he'd done it again: there was no film in the camera.

Early in July 1945, Les and I were among the troops—mostly of the 8th Infantry Regiment—being transported from Le Havre, France, to New York on the *USS Hermitage*. We were both assigned to get material for the ship's newspaper, called *The Scuttlebutt*. Acting as the inquiring reporter, Les concocted a loaded question for each day of the trip. One that I remember went something like this: "Tell me soldier, what was the very worst experience you ever had with an officer?"

Back in the states and out of the Army, Les decided he would engage in a bit of journalism to support himself while he put the finishing touches on The Big One. The Big One, the book he had been writing throughout his army career, was a batch of a thousand or more manuscript pages. With this one it was really going to make it, Bo (a nickname for Bill). Then, with the profits he'd go into the shrimp business or one of the many other strike-it-rich plans he'd told me about in Germany. And after that there would be more books—the real stuff, Bo. Wait and see.

First, as I recall, Les got a job in the New York office of *Look Magazine*. Great, Bo. But presently he told me the bad news. "They bounced me before I got to know where the men's room was." The same thing happened a short time later at the *Chicago Tribune:* hired and fired within a few days.

Although he was 16 years younger, Les looked—as well as talked—like his famous brother Ernest. He'd been on the edges of the literary scene for several years and, for an hour or more, he could charm listeners with his anecdotes and observations—in a barroom such as Tony Kall's, say, or during job interviews. But, as an editor of my acquaintance once said, "Let's face it, Les's stuff wears thin after a while."

Eventually, in the spring of 1952, Les came to Trenton for a brief visit that, as things turned out, lasted five or six months. He was smiling that triumphant smile again; he'd finished The Big One, Bo, and, finally he was on the verge of Really Making It. That mountain of manuscript pages was now in galley-proof form and, with a bit of editing and typo elimination, the book would be ready for publication.

On instructions from his publisher, Les had been sent to Trenton, where he could get some help in the final editing from Sam Cummings. Sam and his wife, the former Lottie Zimba, were the proprietors of a second-hand book store on Front Street. Alerted to the forthcoming arrival of the brother of Ernest Hemingway, the Cummingses made a tentative reservation for the author at the Hotel Stacy-Trent, best place in town. When Les arrived, however, they found the reservation wouldn't be needed. He was carrying clothing, galley sheets, and the like, in a strapped cardboard box, the kind usually used for mailing laundry. His jacket was frayed at the elbows and his pockets were empty.

Sam Cummings, who had done a lot of editing, recovered from the excitement engendered by the visit of a Hemingway when he took a careful look at the galley pages. So did Lottie when the brief visit turned into weeks, then months.

Working over the galleys, Sam did his best to improve the text, but there wasn't much that could be done. At this stage, it was all but impossible to make any major changes.

After the somewhat edited pages were sent off to the publisher, Les remained with the Cummingses—cracking eggs on his forehead each morning for the amusement of the Cummings children (and driving Lottie up the wall with such routines), and joyously heralding the Big Day, Bo, the day when the book would be published.

A week or so before publication date, Les called to say that he had an advance copy. Would I like to see it? We had lunch in the back room of Tony Kall's and there I got my first look at *The Sound of the Trumpet*. I was in the book, Les had been saying and, thumbing through the pages, I found that, indeed, I was. In the early pages, I noticed, I was Jim or Jimsox Doyle. Toward the end I had become Bill Doyle. Oh well. So we had another beer.

Publication Day finally arrived and so did the reviews. They were all bad. The Big One wasn't going to be so big: it was not, after all, going to take Les out of that huge shadow of his brother. The review that hurt Les the most appeared in *Time*. The reviewer said that the book proved that under certain circumstances some publishers would publish anything—something like that—but mostly what this book proved was "the importance of being Ernest." Zap!

Les went on to a second marriage and to the writing of four more novels. All of them were panned by reviewers and none made any money. Les, however, finally did make a big score with a book that he said was his birthright. It would be titled *My Brother Ernest Hemingway*. Les would still be in that big shadow, but at long last he would have a best-seller, and with the royalties, Bo, just watch!

In the early 60s—1962 I think it was—I remember talking with Les several times when he was putting together the book. I especially remember one day at lunch in New York, seeing a letter he had just received from Ernest, then living in Cuba. Somebody had told Les that the appeal of the book would be greatly hyped if he could include some of the letters Ernest had written, especially some of the "angry" ones he had sent to his parents from Paris in the 1920s. Les had access to some of them and, until receiving Ernest's letter from Cuba, he intended to include them, verbatim. I can't recall Ernest's exact words in that letter but he made it clear that Les was not to use any of the letters at all and at one point allowed as how he was certain that no Hemingway would ever stoop to blackmail to get what he wanted.

Les solved the problem by changing the lines of the letters from the first to the third person and thus was able to include the kind of inside stuff that made the book sell.

And sell it did, in full length and in pieces. From *Playboy* alone he got something like $27,000 for a few chapters. In all, he made about $92,000, a tidy sum in those days of 5% mortgage interest.

In the ensuing years Les continued to write but, as things were to turn out, he never again came up with a winner. Even so, he wasn't down yet.

One day when I was wondering what old Les Hemingway, my Fourth Division accomplice, was doing with all that dough, I got a letter from him. Headed, as usual, with something like "Greetings, Old Krautland Buddy," the letter contained some exciting news. At least Les was excited. He had, somewhere about six miles off the southeast coast of Jamaica, found an undersea mountain and, Bo, listen to this: he was going to convert it into nothing less than his own damned country, a brand-new nation and it was going to be called New Atlantis! I forget the rest of the letter, but it was clear that Les was riding high again, surer now than ever before of stepping out of the shadow he never mentioned.

Eventually *The New York Times,* and hundreds of other papers, ran AP and UPI stories about Ernest Hemingway's brother's fantastic project. In a letter from Les, I received occasional progress reports. With what was left of that $92,000, he was towing junked railroad freight cars and a lot of other massive hunks of junk out to sea and getting it into place over that undersea mountain—making fantastic progress, Bo, and before you knew it, he'd have that mountain above sea level and he'd start building the most fantastic bistros, bordellos and gambling casinos in all of this blue-eyed world. Wait and see. His letters at times appeared to ooze with anticipation. In one of them he asked if I would be interested in being appointed Ambassador from New Atlantis to the United Nations. He was serious. In another he included sheets of postage stamps—New Atlantis stamps he'd had printed.

Finally, the big day was about to arrive—the day when New Atlantis would formally become a sovereign nation. I was invited to participate in the ceremony. So was Sam Cummings, who had been offered some such title as Secretary of State. Sam and I were tempted for a while; it sounded, uh, interesting. For some reason, however—probably the size of the air fare—we decided not to go.

A wise decision, as things were to turn out, for despite all Les's efforts, all the tugboat-carted load of junk, the waves kept washing away the foundation of New Atlantis and with it Les's dream.

From time to time after that I would get word of Les. He was conducting fishing tours in and around Key West. He was doing some PR for a jai alai center in Tampa. In his final years, Les was, of course, still writing, but now it was for his newsletter about fishing in the Miami area.

No more shots at the Big Score. No way out of that shadow. But in the final moment of his life Les, at long last, succeeded in emulating his big brother. This is how it was reported the other day:

MIAMI BEACH, Fla.—Leicester Hemingway apparently took his own life like his brother Ernest and their father. He was 67.

Hemingway, in poor health, was found dead Monday of an apparently self-inflicted gunshot wound to the head . . . .

Personal Notes:
Clinical Depression Waylays Unsuspecting Stroke Victim
The Times, Sunday, Feb. 13, 1993

I couldn't sleep, day or night, for two weeks or more. I had no appetite at all; at dinner I waited until my wife, Marge, left the room and I wrapped, say, a piece of chicken in a napkin and hid it in my pocket.

I didn't want to get out of bed in the morning. I had to force myself to take a shower. Several times I checked my weight on the bathroom scale: 148 down from 167! I looked at myself in the mirror. I looked like one of the prisoners I had seen at Dachau. Still I couldn't force myself to eat.

I checked *The Times* and *The New York Times* each morning and found nothing of interest. Alone, I let the telephone ring unanswered. When a neighbor asked if I'd like to walk with him to the post office, I made my excuses and returned to the lounge chair to try, once again, to fall asleep.

I played solitaire until I was sick of it. I tried to write in my journal, but, day after day, the best I could do was one sentence or a variation of it: "I feel like going to sleep and never waking up."

But at night, the endless night, I just stared into the dark or closed my eyes in another fruitless attempt at sleep. During the day, though I was weak with fatigue, I could not nap, for even a few minutes.

One day I looked into a book Marge had brought from the library: *How to Cope with Depression* (from the Johns Hopkins Center for Affective Disorders], by Drs. J. Raymond DePaulo Jr. and Keith Russell Ablow. On page 21 I found a list of symptoms:

1. Depressed mood.
2. Markedly diminished interest or pleasure in almost all activities.

3. Significant weight loss or weight gain.
4. Increased sleep or inability to sleep.
5. Slowed movements on inability to sit still.
6. Fatigue or loss of energy.
7. Feelings of worthlessness or excessive guilt.
8. Diminished ability to think or concentrate.
9. Recurrent thoughts of death or suicide.

I had all of the above!

I could not go on like this!

I read the first one: "No one is to blame. Just as a diabetic cannot, by will power alone, control his or her blood sugar, a person with depression cannot simply decide to elevate his or her mood. Norman Cousins notwithstanding, it would be foolhardy to depend solely on a mind-over-matter approach to a disease. Knowing this should help release those with depression from the painful suspicion, which some harbor, that what really lies behind their illness is a personal failure or weakness. Personal strength can't, by itself, change the genes a person has inherited or the stroke a person has had."

Or the stroke a person has had. It happened to me about 9 o'clock, Tuesday night, October 19. I had played golf that afternoon at the Lawrenceville School course—43 for nine holes. After dinner, Marge was reading a book to me—a usual nightly occupation. It was Edith Wharton's *The Age of Innocence*: "Newland Archer arrived at the Chiverses' on Friday evening, and on Saturday went conscientiously through all the rites appertaining to a weekend at Highbank."

Suddenly I'd had enough of Edith Wharton. I asked Marge to stop reading and in doing so I slurred my speech. I felt tired and weak. "Think I'll go to bed." I fell asleep almost immediately.

The next morning I woke up to find that I was slurring my speech even more and I was feeling flat, tired, blah. At the Medical Center at Princeton I learned, after being examined by Dr. Ian Livingstone, that I had had a stroke. A minor stroke. My mother had died of a stroke at 74. My sister Adele (Gill) had died of a stroke in her 50s. But mine was only a minor one. Not to worry. I could probably look forward to almost complete recovery. Many people had made almost miraculous recoveries. For some reason, perhaps because I was discharged from the hospital after only two days, I anticipated recovery within a few days.

A few days later I was hitting golf balls on Lawrenceville's practice fairway. A few days after that I was hitting tennis balls with Marge. I made contact with the ball, but I couldn't hit straight. Though I aimed at the middle of the court, the balls kept going left and out of the court.

Oh, well, I thought, with practice I'd be hitting them straight in a few days. And I'll be back on the golf course with Brendan Byrne and JP Miller, and winning quarters from both of them.

I didn't know that clinical depression often accompanied a stroke. I didn't know much about depression. And I certainly did not consider myself a candidate for it.

Within a short time, I would learn that I was.

[After what seemed like a long haul, Bill pulled out of the depths of his depression with the help of Prozac. I remember the day it happened. We were riding somewhere in our car. I was driving and he was telling me about something he had read that was quite funny and had gotten him to laughing. He started laughing again as he told me, laughing so hard that he doubled over in the passenger's seat. It was so infectious that I laughed too. "Why am I laughing," he sputtered, "when my life has turned to shit?" We both realized that he had turned a corner and was on the way back to his old self. We both felt incredible relief.

Although the depression had lifted, the residual effects of the stroke hadn't. They were quite minimal however, but were obvious in his altered penmanship, and slightly slower speech.

Bill had always been a great story teller with just the right amount of understatement, ending up with a good punch. The trademarks of the good journalist he was. He writes about the change and what it means to him in the following essay written in June 1994, six months after the stroke.]

Learning humility. Learning empathy for stutterers and fat people, social phobics, people with skin disorders or facial tics, the girl nobody asks to dance, people who are just out of the mainstream—the others, the nerds . . . . All this as a result of a stroke. Now I know how the other half lives. I am there.

I used to be able to tell about living with Hemingway during World War II, or traveling in Europe after the war, writing for the *Feed Bag Journal, The Bible of the Animal Food Industry,* losing a room to 11 puppies in Tangier, living in the hotel on appetizers, etc. So it was only natural that I would try again after the stroke to mesmerize my audience. Speaking of such and such, once upon a time . . . I would start haltingly while I got my esses articulated. But you get stopped as you notice your friends wandering off, their eyes glazing over before you've finished the first sentence. Before you know it, someone breaks in about a car they just bought, a dull story that steals your thunder, and there's nothing you can do about it. You are stuck, and you learn to endure something that the stutterers and the fat and timid have been putting up with their whole lives. Not only do you learn to endure but you also learn to survive and laugh at yourself and the world, too. If old age is not for sissies, then one must develop a sense of humor.

Suddenly you find yourself alone with no one listening to you, two or three conversations going along happily; you look left and right and find no one listening or even including you in the conversation. Oh well, have another drink, peanut, or chocolate mousse pie while your wife isn't looking. Now you can become a keen observer of the scene, like Woody Allen's quintessential loser. Just what is so fascinating about the story that guy just told . . . you ponder.

Now you know how some people feel all their lives. Like a wallflower. All the others at a cocktail party chattering happily away, and you're stuck with some terrific tales but no one wants to listen.

"Did you know that Schmeling . . . ?" At the first slurred *ess* you notice others drifting away. If you are new in the group, you try to explain,

"Please pardon my speech, I've had a stroke," but you still lose them.

They are already looking elsewhere for conversation. You try: "Did you ever know what happened in the 1904 Olympics" . . . but they're straying already . . . too many "s" sounds. Or you try: Speaking of this, one day that happened . . . but you're too late.

Then you remember P.W. that strange little guy in your high school class who lisped. He was skinny and ugly and too officious to make up for all he lacked. Now I have new respect for the P.W.'s of the world. It almost makes having a stroke something wonderful. It adds a new dimension to me, something I would not have wanted to miss.

JP Miller, Reviewing the Life of Writer—and Friend, *The Times,* November, 11, 2001

One afternoon in 1954, JP (James Pinckney) Miller set off for Manhattan from his apartment in Manhasset, Queens. He was carrying a copy of *Hide and Seek*, a television script he had written while trying to make ends meet as an air-conditioning refrigeration salesman.

Arriving at NBC-TV, he was asked if he had an appointment. Of course, he lied: he had an appointment with Terry Lewis Robinson. Robinson was script editor for Fred Coe, the producer of *Philco Playhouse*. But she was apparently out to lunch.

What to do?

While trying to decide, JP encountered Bob Costello in the hall, a former classmate at the Yale Drama School and now Robinson's assistant. Jim asked if he would please give his script to Robinson. Sorry, Costello said, but unsolicited material was not accepted. Well, Jim asked, how was an unknown ever going to be read?

Costello eventually relented. He directed Jim to Robinson's empty office and told him to leave his script on her desk. Jim placed it on top of a pile of scripts. It was a tall pile and a very long shot.

About a week later he got a phone call from a woman with a gruff voice. She'd read his play and wanted to know the name of his agent. It was Robinson. Jim said he didn't have an agent. How did the play get to her desk? He told her he'd put it there. Well, she said she'd read it, liked it and wanted to buy it. Some weeks later, *Hide and Seek* was aired, a story about an old blind woman in the South and her grandson, an orphan—with Arthur Penn directing and Mildred Dunnock playing the grandmother. The reviews were good, and Jim's days as a salesman were over. But along the way to *Days of Wine and Roses*, his greatest hit, there were to be some bumps in the road.

The final bump in the road, for Jim's many friends and admirers, was his death at age 81, on October 31, after five weeks of illness. It was hard to believe that the big, swashbuckling Texan was gone. The boxer known as Tex Frontier in his late teens (until one night he forgot to duck). The poet and novelist in the black cowboy hat. The host of sumptuous dinners, lovingly prepared by his French wife, Liane, at his home near Stockton where you would meet the likes of S. J. Perelman or Mitch Miller or Eli Wallach. The teller of X-rated jokes. The outspoken liberal writing passionate letters to the editor. The avid golfer and tennis player. The naval officer aboard aircraft carriers in World War II who was awarded a Purple Heart and a Bronze Star. The proud and loving father of six children.

At lunch on September 21, the day after my 85th birthday, in Lawrenceville's Acacia Restaurant, Jim had been, as usual, full of life, at his best swapping favorite poems with former Gov. Brendan Byrne, trading stories with Jerry ("Adam Smith") Goodman and me. We laughed and joked for more than two hours.

During Jim's burial service last Sunday at Mount Hope Cemetery on a sunny hill overlooking Lambertville, I finally began to accept the fact that our bigger-than-life friend of more than three decades was gone. In his eulogy at the grave, Byrne covered the highlights of Jim's life, even recalling what he would say after belting a long drive down the center of the fairway: "I didn't get all of it." Then, as the casket was lowered, Jim's wife, Liane, uttered something that we all will long remember: "Good night, my sweet cowboy!" After a slight pause, she added: "I said that every night."

At the cemetery and later in the crowded rooms of the Swan Hotel in Lambertville, friends recalled how much they enjoyed Jim's books, especially *Liv* and *The Skook*, along with such teleplays and movies as *The Rabbit Trap*, the Emmy-winning *The People Next Door*, and, of course, *Days of Wine and Roses*. I remembered Jim's telling me how, after some rough times, he came to write it: "After an unpleasant experience in Hollywood, I came back to New York, thinking I'd sell my house in Manhasset, buy a boat and become a fisherman in Riverhead, Long Island. To hell with writing. But one day in Manhattan I bumped into Fred Coe of the *Philco Playhouse* days, and he said he'd been looking all over for me. He was doing three plays for *Playhouse 90*. Would I be interested? 'No,' I said, 'I'm through, sick of it all.' Coe said, 'If you change your mind, Pappy, give me a call. Put your idea in two sentences and it's a go.'

"I went home, started drinking and got completely smashed, couldn't sleep and started thinking about an uncle of mine who was a drunk. Then the story popped into my head. It was 2 a.m., but I called Coe. 'Here it is,' I said. 'It's about two people, attractive and nice, who love to drink and fall in love. They keep on drinking till the bottle becomes more important to them than they are to each other.' Coe said, 'I like it, Pappy. Go ahead and write it.'"

Jim did, and as they say, the rest is history. On one of the proudest nights of his life, the 25th anniversary dinner of Alcoholics Anonymous, he was honored for the many who joined that organization after seeing *Days of Wine and Roses*.

Dwyer Addictions,
Undated personal essay

My Dad never got over the wonder of television. "Just imagine," he would say, "here I sit in my living room in Trenton, New Jersey, and I can see the Yankees play in Detroit, and I can hear even a foul tip. Or I can have a fifty-yard line seat at the Super Bowl or a front seat at Kennedy's inauguration, all in my living room."

When there were only 50,000 television sets in the whole USA—or was it 500,000—my Dad had an Emerson, and later a Philco with a 12-inch screen. The night when I returned home after spending a year as a roving correspondent in Europe and North Africa, I realized how addicted he really was. It was the spring of 1951. When I rang the front-door bell, Mom answered and welcomed me with her usual warm greeting. Meanwhile Dad remained in his wing chair in front of the TV. Now it was an RCA Victor with an 18-inch screen. I took a seat and had my first glimpse of Milton Berle—Uncle Miltie, in the popular Texaco show. Dad had said a brief hello to me but remained in the wing chair watching Uncle Miltie's antics. Mom presently returned with some brownies and took her seat after offering them to Dad and me.

She didn't remain quiet for long. "Oh, for heaven's sake, Ed, can't we turn that thing off?"

"Just a minute," Dad said. "It'll be over in a minute or two."

But this wasn't good enough for Mom. She got up, walked to the TV and snapped it off. "Now," she said, turning to me, "tell us all about Paris and London and all the rest."

I happened to mention that one day aboard the *France*, the ship that carried me home, there had been exceptionally rough seas. Dishes and glasses were knocked to the floor.

"Rough seas!" Dad said. "I'll bet it wasn't as rough as the time your mother and I took the night boat to Boston." Once more, despite protests from Mother, I was to hear the details of that unforgettable trip to Boston.

Dad was glued to the TV set when, some years later, I returned from Glassboro State College, the scene of a Summit meeting between Premier Aleksei Kosygin of the Soviet Union and President Lyndon B. Johnson. I figured he had to have seen some of the extensive news coverage.

Apparently not.

"Well," he said, greeting me at the door. "Where've you been?"

"Glassboro with the Governor."

"What've you been doing down there?"

I entered and proceeded to tell him about my big day. But I didn't get very far. Dad had enjoyed a far bigger day on television.

Shaking his head, Dad said, "Well, all I can say is that you and the Governor missed one hell of a ball game: the Yankees beat Detroit, four to nothing. And the TV was so clear I could hear the ball hit the catcher's mitt."

Over the years, except for Glassboro, there wasn't much that Dad missed while seated in his front-row TV chair. Usually, along with Mom, he took in such standards as *Toast of the Town* with Ed Sullivan, *Twenty-One* with Charles Van Doren, among others, plus, of course, local boy Ernie Kovacs. Dad was right there when Jack Kennedy debated Richard Nixon, when John Glenn became the first American to orbit the earth, when Jackie Kennedy gave her White House tour, when Pope John XXIII convened Vatican II, as well as when just about any major sports event was on the tube. And he never ceased to marvel at the magic of it all.

Dad died in 1970, before the Age of the Computer. For a dozen years or more I decided that I, like many a Luddite, could get along without a computer. The old IBM Selectric typewriter was far better for me, I thought. In the 1970s and 1980s I completed two books with the Selectric while working full-time as a columnist. Who needed a computer?

Early in 1995 my wife, Marge, maker of most of the big decisions in the Dwyer household, decided it was time to enter the computer world. I had had a stroke in October 1993. At the time I was writing columns on the Selectric, sometimes rewriting them four or five times before getting the spelling et cetera right. But I insisted the typewriter was the only way, especially for an old geezer like me. A few months later, I lost the sight in my right eye and I knew my days with the Selectric were about to end.

Our first computer was an Apple. It was so easy to operate that even I could manage it within a few weeks. Correcting typos was no longer a problem. No more retyping of columns. In short order, I was in love with the Apple.

In 1997 we graduated to a Dell V400c, complete with Fax, and I was really hooked. With one touch of a Start button, my column was off to *The Times* in Trenton. Letters flew to their destinations via the fax machine.

After resisting it for a year or more, I succumbed to e-mail. But what a wonder I found it to be. With just one click of the Reply button, additional column notes moved instantly from Lawrenceville to Trenton. With another click I was in touch with daughter Suzy at St. Mark's School near Boston, where she was teaching English. With further clicks I was in touch with my golfing buddies. Imagine! I was just as hooked on the computer as Dad had been on television.

Addiction seems to run in the family.

Golfing with Dad,
New Jersey Golf Magazine, October, 2004,
Bill's last work in print, age 87

"What say?" Dad said to me, "You want to make yourself a shiny silver dollar this afternoon?"

It was Saturday morning, and the questions meant just one thing: Dad was going to give golf another try, this time on a Saturday afternoon when the course was sure to be crowded. I'd hoped to go canoeing on the Delaware River with the guys that afternoon, and the last thing I wanted to do was to caddy for him, as I had reluctantly done a couple times before. There were some things Dad just didn't get about golf, and one of them was that you didn't bring along your own caddie; you hired one of the regular caddies.

But at age thirteen I found it difficult to explain some things to Dad.

As he had more than once recalled, when *he* was a boy, that was back around 1900, he was paid exactly one dollar for a whole week of delivering drugs for Long's Pharmacy in Trenton—and, by God, he had to supply his own bicycle for the job. Now here was a chance for me to earn a dollar for just carrying a golf bag for a few hours. It made perfect sense to him, especially at the time of the Great Depression that everybody was talking about.

It was about a thirty-minute drive from our summer bungalow in Washington's Crossing, New Jersey, to the Hopewell Valley Golf Club. The bungalow was just a brassie shot or two from where Washington landed after crossing the Delaware on Christmas night in 1776. (The next day, Washington's Continentals saved the Revolution by routing the Hessians in the Battle of Trenton.)

So here we were, father and son, approaching the first tee of the Hopewell Valley course. I was carrying Dad's bag of clubs, a small canvas one, not at all like the leather bags the others were using. I was sure some of the others were noticing the difference, even the caddies.

The area around the tee was crowded with men—no women were allowed on Saturdays—waiting their turn. After hitting their drives, four men and their caddies, all regular caddies, would head toward the creek that meandered through the approach to the first green. Minutes later, when they reached the creek, another foursome would tee off. So it went for a long time, but the crowd waiting to play never diminished.

With his driver in hand, Dad was meanwhile trying to find a place in one of the foursomes. "Say, fellas," he would say to some men waiting near, "you need a fourth?" But there were no takers; their foursomes were already made up—or so they said.

I went over to a bench in the shade and away from a couple of caddies who seemed to be staring at me, and smirking. What was I doing here anyway? I thought as I sat down. Why had I gone along with this? Next time . . . no, there wouldn't be any next time.

I followed Dad with my eyes as he persisted in his search, only to be turned down by one group after another. At one point I winced as he seemed about to approach some younger men, thirtyish and wearing natty golf gear. Oh, no, was he going to ask them, too? He was indeed, and they laughed as they turned him down.

Shortly after, they passed my way and I heard one of them say, "Who was that old duffer?"

"I have no idea," came the answer. "But did you ever see an outfit like that before?"

Damn smart-alecks, I mumbled, but for the first time I took a good look at Dad's getup. Unlike the stylish plus-fours that most of the others sported, he was wearing white duck knickers that barely reached his kneecaps. And white sneakers, not golf shoes. I laughed to myself, and immediately felt guilty about it and even worse because now I was beginning to hope that he would never find anybody at all to play with.

My hopes (as well as my guilty feeling) rose as Dad came toward the bench where I was sitting. He sat down next to me and said, "This place is just too crowded today." There was a lengthy pause; I couldn't think of anything to say. Then, smiling, he turned to me and said, "How about if you and I give that miniature course a try?"

"That Tom Thumb we passed on the way here?" I said.

"Yeah, how about it?"

"Well, sure."

Using nothing but putters, we played all eighteen holes of the little course.

It was fun.

PART IV

The Endgame

Bill died on March 22, 2005, nineteen days after he walked into Princeton hospital feeling fine. Two days before he was moved to Cardiac Care because of a chest pain, he was listening with headphones to jazz singer Blossom Dearie, tapping the beat with his fingers—engaged right to the end.

On March 26th we held a going-way party for Bill in his beloved garden at our home. Our good friend and neighbor, journalist John Timpane, read my remarks after a musical interlude of Oscar Peterson's rendition of "Satin Doll":

> When I first met Bill, I was enchanted with his extraordinary sense of play. He was 43, a charming and worldly ex-war correspondent, I, a naïve, 23-year-old would-be starlet. I thought he was the funniest man I had ever met. He thought I was beautiful and very special. Hey, that worked for me.
>
> His offbeat sense of humor blended perfectly with mine. Most people who knew us thought we were nuts, so we kept our plans secret. During our three-month whirlwind courtship, he

sent countless letters to my workplace at New Jersey Manufacturers, addressing them to the "spectacular" or "marvelous" or "beautiful and fabulous" Miss Marjorie Elizabeth Wright. On one card he sent, a woman was featured dangling from her toes by a thread. On this he wrote: "Courage, help is coming." On Dwyer Brothers stationery another letter started: "Dear Miss Wright: Congratulations on your recent engagement. Please come in to Dwyer Brothers and select your new stationery from our fine collection."

One morning, he called me at work and said he had car trouble. Could he borrow my car? It was an old 1953 Chevy Bel Air two-door coupe. He'd bring it back by lunch. I met him outside the office door with the keys. He wore his signature outfit: tweed jacket, blue button-down shirt, khakis or corduroys, and always a hat worn at a rakish angle. He stole a kiss in the sunlight and sauntered off in that ever-jaunty walk.

When I went out to get the car at lunch, there it was: a shiny, newly-painted blue gem. He later explained that it was getting rusty, so he'd taken it to the one-hour specialist, Earl Schibe, for $39.99. This in lieu of diamonds and flowers, of course.

"Ya know," I said to him once," other guys called me beautiful, but I always knew it was a line. When you said it, I actually believed you. And that's probably why we're together." He said, with a wink, "Marge, mine was a line, too. I was just better at it."

Our life together for the next 43 years continued in this tradition. From beginning to end, Bill was all vitality, vigor, and delight in chaos. When nearby, he was either talking or whistling—or adding more papers to the general disorder of our home. He was in a constant race against time to accomplish what he wanted to write. He seemed to work best in clutter. (I shouldn't have been surprised. When I first met him, he drove an out-of-date two-tone DeSoto, backseat filled with faded old newspapers he needed for some project or other.) Once a houseguest took me aside, when she saw Bill's columns spread out on the kitchen floor, and other items covering all horizontal surfaces, and said: "Marge, I would be institutionalized if I lived like this." Eventually, we were able to contain Bill and his world to one room. Still, it was a constant struggle to keep the books and papers and notes from spilling out.

His curiosity about life and all its possibilities made him a wonderful lifetime companion. Not that this did not lead to occasional problems. The minute I announced that dinner would be on the table in five minutes, he'd decide to cut the grass. When I threw out his worn-out clothes, he'd retrieve them from the garbage can, saying, "I can use these when I'm painting," which he never did. On those rare occasions when he picked up a paint brush, invariably he was wearing his best clothes.

His motto could have been a saying he often quoted: "Chance favors the prepared mind." He was always where things were happening, and he had a knack for jumping on opportunities. You have to be ready. You have to accept life on its terms. This attitude led to many adventures, including his European tour with Eleanor Roosevelt, his five-month stay in Copenhagen with a bunch of jazz musicians. Speaking of jazz, only Bill would call classical radio station 89.1 and ask them to play more Dixieland.

Bill on tour with Eleanor Roosevelt, late '50s

He was a guy who loved variety and diversity. In his various journalistic efforts over many years for the *Trentonian* and the *Trenton Times,* Bill reached a wide readership, the whole range of our society, industry leaders and waitresses and laborers, everyday people who recognized him from his picture. "Hey, whaddya know?" he'd report to me with pride as he returned the garbage cans to the garage. "The garbage man reads my column."

In other words, Bill had a great taste for chance and its blessings. When in 1971, after being childless for almost a decade, we saw our daughter Suzy come into the world, I could tell he shared my sense that we were blessed. And again when Suzy and her husband, Andrew Harrison, presented us with our two dear grandchildren, Hall and Charley, Bill was filled with wonder and love.

He had rejected organized religion and yet was the most godly of men. He believed in human rights and justice for all and lived that belief every day. After the Newark riots, convinced that writing was the key, and after putting in a full day as Press Secretary to Gov. Richard J. Hughes of New Jersey, he caught a train and taught journalism at night in a storefront on Newark's Springfield Avenue.

A decorated veteran of World War II, he loved his country and the principles on which it was founded so much, he had to protest when he felt his government was veering off course. Bill was passionate about his causes, whether it meant marching in Washington against the Vietnam War, picketing for peace against the invasion of Kuwait and later Iraq, or befriending someone whom others mistreated. He had little tolerance for man's inhumanity to man, welfare for the rich, or what he saw as wrongheaded politicians. He awakened in me a social conscience, and I am simply a better person because of him.

He wasn't always perfect. I wasn't always perfect, and our marriage wasn't always perfect. That's for sure. But our last years were as good as the first, if not better. We shared the quieter things: Scrabble and walks, reading together, intimate gatherings with friends and family, and personal moments of exquisite sweetness. In essence, he was what he often called someone he admired greatly: a rare bird. He had a marvelous life surrounded by love from many different sources. He defied death during the war. He nearly died from a bee sting 25 years ago. He battled back after a stroke a decade ago. And for the last two years, he had to endure an esophagus that wanted to close up and repeated procedures to open it.

Last Tuesday, all that luck and pluck and energy came to a close. Today, I have nothing but gratitude for my life with Bill, but, until the day I die, I will miss his vital presence in my life, and the steady, warm comfort of my hand in his.

Marge and Bill Dwyer, Christmas 1966

Many months after Bill died, I found this reverie he had written long before. I like to think he called these moments back as the morphine drip passed him from this world to the next.

Moments to Put in a Jar and Keep Forever
as Francie mused in Betty Smith's *A Tree Grows in Brooklyn*

Sights and sounds of home.

Children's voices from up the street. The cracking sound of a squirrel in a crabapple tree. Pieces of shells falling to the ground. Dogs barking in the direction of Main Street.

Sounds. Dazey, chin on forepaws, stretched out, her ears picking up the squirrel sounds, her eyes seeking but not finding the squirrel. Dazey suddenly running off, barking in the direction of the barking. The squeaking of a dove taking sudden flight. Up high a jet tearing through the air. Birds coming and going, cawing and shrilling of a dozen birds. Two low-flying planes buzzing by. A truck grunting down the street. Cricket and other sounds in the background.

Sights. The gnarled arms of the crabapple tree against the white house with pale blue shutters. The green and white director's chairs on the sun-spackled stones of the terrace. Dazey back and sprawled out next to the house. The shades of green: rhododendrons, laurel, peach tree, graceful hemlocks, the boxwood. The blue spruce, the white-thighed birches, the lavender blossoms of the green edging of the formal garden.

LaVergne, TN USA
20 September 2009
158443LV00002B/123/P